The Americans with Disabilities Act

Its Impact on Libraries

The Library's Responses in "Doable" Steps

ALA Association of Specialized
and Cooperative Library Agencies
Preconference

San Francisco Marriott Hotel
Friday, June 26, 1992

Joanne L. Crispen, Editor

Association of Specialized
and Cooperative Library Agencies
a division of the American Library Association
Chicago 1993

Cover and text designed by Donavan Vicha

Composed by ALA Production Services in Bookman Light and Bodoni using Ventura Publisher 3.0. Camera-ready pages output on a Varityper VT600 laser printer

Printed on 50-pound Finch Opaque, a pH-neutral stock, and bound in 10 pt. C1S cover stock by IPC, St. Joseph, Michigan

The paper used in this publication meets the minimum requirements of American National Standard for Information Sciences— Permanence of Paperfor Printed Library Materials, ANSI Z39.48-1984. ∞

Library of Congress Cataloging-in-Publication Data

The Americans with Disabilities Act : its impact on libraries :
   the library's responses in "doable" steps / editor, Joanne L.
   Crispen
      p.   cm.
  ISBN 0-8389-7636-0
  1. Libraries and the handicapped— United States— Congresses.
I. Crispen, Joanne L.
Z711.92.H3A4   1993
027.6′63— dc20   92-37146

Copyright © 1993 by the American Library Association. All rights reserved except those which may be granted by Sections 107 and 108 of the Copyright Revision Act of 1976.

Printed in the United States of America.

97 96 95 94 93   5 4 3 2 1

Contents

Acknowledgments   v

Introduction   vii
Duane Johnson

ADA Preconference Committee
Members, Contributors, and Consultants   ix

Opening Remarks   xi
David Esquith

Difficult Times   1
John Wodach

A Historical Overview   9
Mary Lou Breslin

An Administrator's View
of "What Is Doable"   17
Joseph Shubert

Social Implications
for Disabled and Nondisabled People   23
Judith Heumann

Exemplary Library Programs and
Services for Those with Disabilities   27
Phyllis Dalton

Adaptive Technology
to Access Information   34
Leonard Anderson

Making ADA Work   40
Richard Sheppard

Questions and Answers   45

Appendix A   55
    Self-Evaluation Survey

Appendix B   157
    Adaptive Technology Exhibitors

Appendix C   158
    Ten Commandments of Etiquette

Appendix D   159
    Exemplary Library Programs and Services

Appendix E   161
    NIDRR ADA Brochure

Acknowledgments

The effort, thought, and planning of the members of the Association of Specialized and Cooperative Library Agencies, a division of the American Library Association, made the preconference and the publication on the Americans with Disabilities Act possible.

The many contributions of the ASCLA staff should be acknowledged: the advice and knowledge of Andrew Hansen, Executive Director; the sustaining support and initiative of Cheryl Malden, Administrative Secretary; and the ability of Nelle Gerts to cope with a variety of tasks.

The resourcefulness, cooperation, and patience of the ALA Production Services staff, especially Dianne Rooney and Eileen Mahoney, are to be commended.

Joanne L. Crispen

Introduction

Duane Johnson

The subject of this preconference, the ADA, has been the law of the land for two years, but there is a wide gulf between the letter of that law and the reality of the placement of policy and services within the ADA. The experts on hand for this agenda will help us come to an understanding of the how, why, and when of the ADA implementation process.

David Esquith, senior policy analyst for ADA at the Office of Special Education and Rehabilitation Services of the U.S. Department of Education, will be the moderator today.

John Wodach is with the U.S. Department of Justice, Civil Rights Division, and heads the office on the Americans with Disabilities Act. John has been instrumental in helping the U.S. Department of Education get a technical-assistance program there for people to use. He is one of the leading policymakers in Washington on the Americans with Disabilities Act.

Mary Lou Breslin is with the Disability Rights Education Defense Fund. DREDF had a critical and key role in the writing of the ADA. The persons in that organization understand the kinds of demands that people can reasonably place on libraries in terms of implementing the ADA. It's important to have a good understanding of that, and to question those demands, assumptions, and expectations of what the ADA would mean to persons with disabilities.

Joseph Shubert, state librarian and assistant economics commissioner for libraries in New York State, will present the perspective of the library administrator for services to those with disabilities.

Judith Heumann is the vice-president and cofounder of the World Institute on Disability. Judy has been active in the fight for equality for disabled individuals for over twenty years. One of her first battles was when she was denied a position as a public school teacher and filed a lawsuit against the board of education of the city of New York. Subsequently, she was the first person using a wheelchair to be hired to teach in the New York city school system. Judy has also been one of the persons who has played a key role in numerous pieces of legislation, including ADA. In 1990, she became the first recipient of the Henry B. Betts award for her efforts to significantly improve the quality of life for people with disabilities, and Disability Rights Education and Defense Fund.

Phyllis Dalton is a long-time friend of the Association of Specialized and Cooperative Library Agencies. She was copresident when Health and Rehabilitative Library Services (formally Hospital and Institutional Libraries) merged with the Association of State Library Agencies to become ASCLA. Phyllis is the author of a book that addresses the library service needs of the deaf and hearing impaired. She has contributed many articles on the subject of special services to the literature; she has been a pioneer and in fact a revolutionary in the development of services to special populations and to institutions.

Duane Johnson is State Librarian, Kansas State Library, Topeka.

Leonard Anderson is the project director of the Rehabilitation Engineering Center in Wichita Kansas and part of a network of fifteen grantees who provide information, training, and technical assistance to businesses and agencies with duties and responsibilities under the ADA and to people with disabilities who have rights under the act.

Richard Sheppard is from the President's Committee on Persons with Employment Disabilities and will discuss attitudinal issues on the employment of persons with disabilities.

ADA Preconference Committee Members, Contributors, and Consultants

Chairperson

Grace Jean Lyons, Librarian
District of Columbia Public Library
Martin Luther King Memorial Library
901 G St. NW
Washington, DC 20001

Members

Nancy Bolin, Library Consultant
6756 Springing Step
Columbia, MD 21044

John M. Day, Director
Gallaudet University Library
800 Florida Ave. NE
Washington, DC 20002

Duane F. Johnson, State Librarian
Kansas State Library
State Capitol Building
Topeka, KS 66612-1593

Kathleen O. Mayo, Special Services
  Coordinator
Lee County Library System
2050 Lee St.
Fort Myers, FL 33901

Ruth E. O'Donnell, Library Program Specialist
State Library of Florida
500 S. Bronough St.
Tallahassee, FL 32399-0250

Contributors

Leonard L. Anderson
Vice President of Technical Services
2121 N. Old Manor
Wichita, KS 67208

Mary Lou Breslin, Senior Policy Advisor
Disability Rights Education and Defense
  Funds, Inc.
2212 6th St.
Berkeley, CA 94710

Phyllis Dalton, Library Consultant
7090 E. Mescal St., #261
Scottsdale, AZ 85254

David G. Esquith, Senior Policy Analyst
  for ADA
Office of Special Education and
  Rehabilitative Services
U.S. Department of Education
400 Maryland Ave. S.W.
Washington, DC 20202-2572

Judith Heumann
Vice President
World Institute on Disability
510 16th St., Suite 100
Oakland, CA 94612

Richard Sheppard
Manager, Office of Plans, Projects, & Services
1331 F St. N.W., Rm. 308
Silver Spring, MD 20910

Joseph F. Shubert, State Librarian and
  Assistant Commissioner for Libraries
New York State Library
Cultural Education Center, Rm. 10C34
Albany, NY 12230

John Woodach, Director
U.S. Department of Justice, Civil Rights
  Division
Office of Americans with Disabilities Act
P.O. Box 66738
Washington, DC 20035-9998

Consultants

Donald E. Wright, Director
Niles Public Library
6960 Oakton St.
Niles, IL 60714-3025

Sharon D. McFarland
Maryland State Department of Education
Division of Library Development & Services
200 W. Baltimore St.
Baltimore, MD 21201-2500

Opening Remarks

David Esquith

I'm going to be brief and just let you know that this is a timely meeting. I work with the U.S. Department of Education National Institute on Disability and Rehabilitation Research. These are difficult and exciting times as they relate to the ADA. The panel this morning is going to elaborate on that.

A year from now when there may be another conference on the ADA through your organization, my assumption is you all are going to be doing a lot of talking to each other on how to implement the ADA. Those agencies with technical assistance responsibilities and enforcement responsibilities are really overwhelmed by the ADA, and I think everyone is feeling a little overwhelmed. If you are feeling overwhelmed, that's a pretty reasonable place to be at this point.

The ADA is going to create new solutions to old problems, and part of the spin-off benefit to everyone is increased cooperation among agencies, among libraries, among anyone who has anything to do with the ADA. I hope that you all will take an open-minded questioning posture toward these deliberations.

It will be important for you all to hear from each other. Both the questions that you have about the ADA, as well as some solutions that you are making to get those problems solved. Ultimately, I hope that the solutions that you all come up with are disseminated widely across the country. Issues that relate to the ADA and libraries are common ones, and my office and our technical-assistance centers get questions from people that use libraries and are working in libraries about the ADA and how to make it work successfully.

The following articles are a good starting point for all of us to get a basic understanding of the ADA, lay some basic questions on the table, try to get some answers, and then plan to get more detailed answers to those questions disseminated among all of us.

David Esquith is Senior Policy Analyst for ADA, Office of Special Education and Rehabilitation, U.S. Department of Education.

Difficult Times

John Wodach

I'm delighted to be here to be able to talk with you about the Americans with Disabilities Act, or ADA. I'd like to give you basically a primer on what the ADA stands for, what the requirements of the law are, and the regulations.

I will start with the disclaimer that I've been known to fill up many hours talking about the ADA. My hero in speech making is Fidel Castro, but I will try to keep myself in check and hit the highlights for you.

The ADA is a very comprehensive, very complicated statute. Any time you get five hundred lawyers in a room and ask them to write a paper or a piece of legislation, you get something like this ADA. And I mean that kindly, being one of them.

First of all, the ADA is a civil rights statute, and it's a comprehensive civil rights statute. It's one that delineates responsibilities for wide-ranging entities in this country, and it's one that lays out rights for persons with disabilities in the United States. It has been called the Emancipation Proclamation for persons with disabilities.

Much of the time, people approach laws dealing with disabilities from the perspective that this is something we are doing because it's a good thing to do, it's a form of charity.

The ADA, like the Rehabilitation Act before it, Title 5 of the Rehabilitation Act, is different than that. It's a civil rights law; it has roots in the struggles of African-Americans and women for federal laws that protect their rights. It follows in those footsteps.

What Congress basically did when they started down the road on ADA was to look at existing federal civil rights laws that gave protection for women and for minorities and to compare those with the laws that exist for persons with disabilities.

Basically, they did a simple grid. They superimposed the two, one on top of the other, and saw that there were holes in the fabric of protection for persons with disabilities. The ADA really is an attempt to fill in those holes. So it's comprehensive in its scope.

I'm going to go through the titles (there are four titles that have some relevance to you in the administration of library programs), give you an idea of what the law is about, and give you some indication of how it can apply to you. What I'm going to do is talk about what it requires, and when I finish that I will talk about how it's enforced.

First title is Title 1, and it deals with employment practices. For those of you who are familiar with Title 7 of the Civil Rights Act of 1964, this is really the analog to that title in the ADA. It goes into effect on July 26 of this year. At that time, it will apply to all employers in this country who have twenty-five or more employees. We are talking about private employers, state and local government agencies, labor unions, employment agencies.

Two years from now, July 26, 1994, the law will ratchet down to all employers with fifteen or more employees. So if you are a private entity or a state or local government with that many employees, then you are covered.

John Wodach is Director, Office of Americans With Disabilities Act, U.S. Department of Justice, Civil Rights Division, Coordination and Review Section.

This is something that is not often realized, because people tend to look at the ADA and say Title 1 is employment. Title 2, which covers all the activities of state and local government agencies, went into effect in January of this year. It covers discrimination on the basis of employment.

So what we have is a situation where, if you are part of a public entity, if you are a librarian as part of a state or local government, all your employment practices are covered now.

If you are a private entity, you will be covered starting in July if you have twenty-five or more employees or are part of a system that has twenty-five or more employees— and two years from now, fifteen or more employees.

All employment practices are covered under both Title 1 and Title 2: job classification, hiring, firing, fringe compensation, fringe benefits, the whole range— all terms, conditions, and privileges of employment.

The law protects persons with disabilities. I won't go into the definition in too much detail. It's important that you know it's a very broad definition. Those of you who are familiar with Section 504, Rehabilitation Act of 1983— the (I suppose for us) granddaddy civil rights statute that deals with disability rights issues— know the definition is adopted from that law.

It is extremely expansive. It includes any person who has a physical or mental impairment that substantially limits one or more of that person's major life activities— someone who has a history or record of that kind of impairment and someone who is regarded as having that kind of impairment. It's important to keep in mind that it's wide ranging and covers people with AIDS. People who test positively for the HIV virus are covered.

This is a civil rights law. It is interpreted expansively and it goes that way in the definition— a person with a disability.

In employment, however, it's a two-step process. To be protected by the statute, you have to be a qualified individual with a disability. The Equal Employment Opportunity Commission (EEOC) has provided guidance under Title 1 in terms of what a qualified individual with a disability is. They lay out a two-step process.

The first step is, not surprisingly, the qualifications for the job, the requisite skill, experience, education, and other job-related requirements. A person must fit those.

In addition, the person must be able to perform the essential functions of the job with or without reasonable accommodation to their disability. You start getting into the legal jargon a little bit here, but it is fairly basic.

The essential functions of the job are those fundamental parts of the job, the reason that the job exists. If someone cannot perform the essential functions of the job, he or she is not a qualified individual, not a qualified individual with a disability, and not protected by the ADA.

The EEOC has gone out of its way in response to questions to point out that you don't have to lower the standards of the job. If it's a clerical position and someone has to type seventy-five words a minute, that's the requirement and that's the essential function of the job. You can apply that to all people who apply for the job.

The key concept that is often talked about in terms of discrimination disability is the phrase *reasonable accommodation*. The statute says you must make reasonable accommodation to the known physical or mental limitations of otherwise qualified applicants and employees, unless the employer can demonstrate that doing so is an undue hardship on the operation of the business. Let me deconstruct that a little bit.

Basically, what is a *reasonable accommodation*? In essence it's any change in the work environment or in the way things are done that enables a person with a disability to perform the essential functions of the job. It may be making the work site accessible. It may be providing modified equipment. Most of the activity occurs in providing or modifying equipment: raised desks, computers, specialized software. Providing an accessible parking space may be a reasonable accommodation.

Job restructuring, which is redistributing nonessential or more general functions among several employees, enables a person with a disability to perform certain activities. It may be changed hours. Something that's new in the ADA that Congress added as reasonable accommodation includes reassignment to a vacant position. If you have an employee who can no longer perform the essential functions of a particular job and there is another position that is vacant where they can perform the essential functions of that job, reasonable accommodation would include offering it to that person as long as it's not an undue hardship.

Which brings us to, what is an *undue hardship*? It is defined as something that is a significant difficulty or expense incurred by the employer. Most of the time, this is a cost analysis, but it doesn't have to be. There may be other factors working that would fundamentally change the operation of the business. It is not required to be done.

The heart of discrimination and nondiscrimination in the employment area is really an individualized assessment. It's not making assumptions about what people can and can't do based on past experience, it's not making assumptions based on job category. You have to look at everything on a case-by-case basis.

Persons have different levels of abilities and different jobs may have different essential functions even within a very similar framework. The whole key to ensuring compliance with the employment provisions is an individualized, case-by-case assessment that looks at both what can be done and what the undue hardships are in the job.

Keep in mind that the ADA is not an affirmative statute, it's a nondiscrimination statute. If you have two people who are qualified for a job and one is more qualified, it is not a violation of the law to hire the more qualified person, even if the other qualified person is a person with a disability.

Another major area is the famed preemployment inquiry prohibition. The statute says it is a violation of the law to make a preemployment inquiry either on a form or in a job interview about whether or not a person has a disability. If you have an application for a library card, you can't say, "Do you have a history of mental illness?" Not that I think that's ever been the case.

You can ask if someone can perform the job. So if you have a job that requires driving from, say, one library to another in a system, that's an essential function of that job. You wouldn't ask, "Do you have epilepsy?" You would say, "Can you drive a car; do you have a driver's license." You can look into the person's record on driving.

Similarly, in the preemployment inquiry, you cannot ask about previous Workman's Compensation history, or a variation of that.

On the other hand, if a person has a known disability, the whole preemployment inquiry is really a protection of people with visible disabilities. The idea being it's not information you need to know. What you need to know is whether or not they can do the job. If, however, you are in an interview situation with someone who has a disability that's apparent, it is not inappropriate to bring it up for discussion. You can say, "I see you are in a wheelchair. Will you need special accommodations in terms of doing the job?" As you know, having a discussion, I think an open and honest discussion, is probably appreciated by the person with the disability in that situation.

You can require post-offer medical examinations. There are many jobs for which a medical examination is required. If you did it before you made the offer, it would really be the same as a preemployment medical inquiry. So what you do under the law is, after you have made an offer, you make a conditional offer. "We will give you the software if you can pass our medical exam."

That is appropriate under certain protection that has to be provided for any information that you obtained in that process. You can do this as long as you do it for all applicants for whatever that job category is.

Once a person is on the job, you can require medical exams and make inquiries about disabilities if they are job related and consistent, which is a whole range of legal issues that have been developed under Title 7, the Civil Rights Act of 1964.

One last issue on employment. An employer may require that an individual not pose what the statute calls a "direct threat to the health or safety of himself or others." This is basically the safety notion. The idea was you don't have to hire someone with narcolepsy to handle power tools if that person could do the essential functions of the job but would pose a threat to himself or to others. There are very stringent requirements in this area. They come out of a Supreme Court decision that involves a person with AIDS, and this issue comes up very often in situations involving AIDS.

We are not dealing with supposition or speculative or remote risk. It's case by case, and you have to really look and see if there is a high probability of substantial harm in order to avail yourself, as an employer, of the direct threats language.

The requirements that I have gone through apply to you whether you are an employer covered under Title 1 of the ADA, or whether you are an employer under Title 2 of the ADA. Those of you who are familiar with Section 504 are recipients of federal funds and are covered by 504. Since the seventies, you have been receiving funds; the employment standards are the same.

What Congress basically did in Title 1 of the ADA was to put the Department of Education's title regulations of Section 504 employment into the statute and apply them to the private and public sector as a whole. If you have been working with this issue under Section 504, there is not a lot of new material for you to learn about in terms of employment discrimination.

On to Title 2. Again, Congress took a look at Section 504 and said Section 504 applies to the programs, activities, and entities that receive federal financial assistance. Many state and local government agencies receive federal funds, but only some of the programs were covered. There is a sort of "Swiss cheese" coverage in state and local government agencies. Those of you who follow civil rights law know the college decision by the Supreme Court in the eighties that significantly narrowed coverage.

Congress, in the Civil Rights Restoration Act of 1988, put coverage back to where it had been before. In the eighties, there was a lot of fluctuation, a lot of uncertainty in terms of who was covered and to what extent.

Title 2 of the ADA says that state and local government agencies are covered in their entirety. For many agencies, this may not mean much of a difference. It may not for library services to the extent that they receive federal funds, but now coverage of the state and local government level is total.

The provisions of what that means are again fairly simple. Congress said to the federal agencies, you should develop regulations for what is discrimination by state and local government agencies. We were told to look at Section 504.

So the regulation that the Department of Justice issued that covers public entities is really a Section 504 regulation sort of cleaned up and streamlined.

There are several basic requirements. The most far-reaching is that all of these laws are forward-looking ones. All new construction must be done in an accessible fashion. If you are building a new building, a new library, an addition to a library, it must be done in an accessible fashion. If you are making an alteration to an existing building, it must be done in an accessible fashion.

What is *accessible fashion*? Under the state or local government agencies, you have a choice of two standards to look at. One is something called the ADA Accessibility Guidelines that were issued a year ago and went into effect last January. For under Title 3, which we will talk about, they are sort of state-of-the-art guidelines of what an accessible facility is. They include specific provisions, with which I'm sure you are probably pretty familiar.

In addition, because a number of these entities covered under Title 2 also receive federal funds and are covered by Section 504, there is a choice. There is something called UFAS. Some of us have been accused of being UFASians, people who watch "Star Trek." The Uniform Federal Accessibility Standards have been in place for a number of years, and it's another set of standards. The state or local government entity has the ability to make a choice on a building-by-building basis as to which standard it's going to follow. For some reason, one may choose one over the other.

This will change in another year or so. Under the ADA, something called the Architectural and Transportation Barriers Compliance Board, the federal agencies who called themselves the access board for obvious reasons, is in the process of issuing a proposed ADA accessibility guideline for state and local government agencies.

If you are interested in this sort of thing and if you have something you want to add in this debate, we hope these standards will be published in the Federal Register for comments in about August. When the comments are received and they are done in final form, they will become the guidelines used by state and local government agencies. There will no longer be a choice between the ADA accessibility guidelines and UFAS. Frankly, we hope in the long run we will have one accessibility standard that is used nationwide by the federal government and is adopted by all state and local government agencies, but that is several years away, even though attempts are being made in both the private sector and public sector to get to that goal.

It's important in new construction or alterations to make sure that the builders, the architects, whoever it is that you deal with, know you have to do this in an accessible fashion and that there are certain standards to be followed in making those changes.

Congress didn't leave out the existing physical plants when they talked about what is accessibility, however. When you figure in accessible design features for new buildings and alterations, the cost is really quite limited. When you are retrofitting existing physical plants in order to try and make them accessible, cost is a much, much bigger item and something you really have to confront. The regulations take that into consideration.

A concept called program accessibility was developed by HEW in the seventies. Section 504 is the section that applies here. Program accessibility is something you talk about when you are dealing with existing facilities. You look at your existing physical plants and ask: What is the program we are offering? In what physical facilities do we offer it? What type of impact does that have on persons with disabilities?

The concept here is that you need not remove every existing architectural barrier in order to make your program successful. You will be able to see that program accessibility is really a compromise approach. Program accessibility would allow a public library in a town with four or five branches of the library to choose a couple of those and offer these to be accessible instead of making the whole system accessible, if in doing that it meets the needs of the population and the distances aren't too great. I think you can see this is not always a popular concept with persons with disabilities.

In Washington, D.C., we have a number of public libraries. Our local public library is part of our community and part of our lives, but it is quite inaccessible. A person with a disability in our area would have to use the main library or another branch. That really isn't exactly equal opportunity because much more of a burden is placed on that disabled person. We would hope over the long run, as time goes by, as alterations are made, that all of the branches are going to be made accessible.

But the ADA, under Title 2, does not require that, as long as the program viewed in its entirety on the whole is accessible. The ADA requires that, if you have existing facilities that have architectural barriers, you do a plan to look at the facilities, do that as part of a self-evaluation and a transition plan. There is a planning requirement we recommend very strongly; the law requires that you involve interested persons, including persons with disabilities in that planning process. You are in the business of providing services to this community. It's important to know how they respond and what's important to them.

The other part of Title 2 deals with communications issues. The law requires that you have an effective communication with persons with disabilities and, where necessary, provide appropriate auxiliary aids. We have an example of a state-of-the-art auxiliary aid at this conference. But that includes a wide range of devices and services that make your programs available to persons with hearing, vision, and speech impairments. It can be materials on tape, materials in braille, books in braille, it can be reading machines, it can be the provision of persons who will assist persons in participating in the program. When we are talking about communication issues, the ADA requirement is that you must provide these as long as doing so is not an undue burden or it does not result in a fundamental alteration of your program activity.

From talking to other people and dealing with library issues, I think the issues around communications are probably much more difficult for the provision of your services than the accessibility issues are. The ADA clearly does not require that you offer every book in your library in braille, but the ADA does not provide specific guidance as to what exactly you have to do. It really is something that you should do as part of your self-evaluation in conjunction with the community in which you provide services and in terms of what resources you have available.

Different types of libraries may choose different ways of providing their services. If you stock many best-sellers in your library, you may choose to have those books available on tape. In the Washington area, the libraries are doing that, not because of the ADA, but because so many people are commuting and spending so much time in their cars. The tape selections in libraries are becoming a very important part.

You need to consider how ADA affects your planning in terms of technology. Libraries are changing. I know this only from casually visiting them. I go to my daughter's high school and see how she interacts in the library with her school librarian. It's a very different experience. A lot of students use computerized technology and CD-ROMs that I don't understand, and she goes and does.

The availability of software and other ways of making those materials available to persons with vision impairments will change. As you decide what it is you are going to do to respond to the ADA, you need to take that into consideration in terms of all of that planning.

The Title 2 of the ADA deals with transportation issues. They don't affect libraries directly, but you should know when you are talking about ADA that it has specific transportation requirements in making transportation systems accessible.

Look at ADA as a whole. The idea was to make jobs available to persons with disabilities, to fix our transportation system so that people can get to work and get home from work, to provide public accommodations that are accessible to persons with disabilities, to enable them to enjoy the fruits of their labor by being able to go to a restaurant or a movie and participate in everyday American life.

It's important to view the ADA from that perspective. We are talking about opening up everyday American life to persons with disabilities. If you were to take the law, more than half of the ADA deals with transportation issues. The requirements are very specific. There are different requirements for inner-city rail, over-the-road buses, subway systems. There are very different requirements in terms of vehicles as well as the stations.

Title 4 is the telecommunications part of the ADA. When we were drafting the ADA, we thought this was going to be one of the most difficult sections of the ADA. The telephone system is, obviously, not very available to persons with speech impairments and people with hearing impairments. The ADA had to open up the telecommunications network system in this country to persons with disabilities who have hearing and speech impairments. What Title 4 requires is that, starting in July of 1993, there will be in the United States a telecommunications relay system. This means that people who use telecommunication devices, TDDs, a variety of types of these machines, will have access to the telephone system network as it exists now through the telephone companies.

A person with a TDD will call a TDD operator who will have a TDD machine and will act as intermediary in the conversation with someone who has a regular voice telephone. So that if you are a library, even if you don't have a TDD, you will be able to receive calls from someone who has a TDD through this relay network.

Similarly, if you have to call someone who has a speech impairment or who has a hearing impairment with a TDD, you will be able to have access to them using your regular telephone system.

It's a simple but revolutionary concept that will change telecommunications in this country. We thought it would be a very difficult situation, but the telephone companies signed on to it very early on. Some states have TDD relay systems, but none of them provide comparable service to persons with hearing and speech impairments, and this system will do that.

Title 3 of the ADA, deals with something called *public accommodations*. Public accommodations is, of course, private entities. So much for truth in advertising, I suppose.

A public accommodation is a private entity that owns, operates, leases, or leases to one of twelve categories of entity types. The most important thing to know is that libraries is one of the twelve categories, so that an entity that is a private entity (perhaps a library) is covered under Title 3 of the ADA.

A library that is a state or local government or otherwise public entity is covered under Title 2 of the ADA. There are some differences between Title 2 and Title 3. The auxiliary aids and communications are almost exactly the same. The new construction and alterations are mostly the same, although there are some additional requirements in the alterations area.

In the new construction alterations area, Title 3 has its most rigorous requirements. Any private entity that is going to build a new building or is going to alter its existing physical plants must do so according to the ADA Accessibility Guidelines. Again, it is the ADA disability guidelines for private entities. Just so you get an idea of the breadth of Title 3, I will go through the categories for you to see what Congress had in mind when we talk about places of public accommodation.

These are places of lodging, hotels, motels, inns, things of that nature, establishments serving food or drink, places of entertainment, theaters, concert halls, sports stadiums, an establishment selling or renting items. This is a very broad category and is often not thought of in terms of other types— retail shops, stores, shopping malls, video stores, bakeries.

Places of public display are libraries. You may be surprised— you may not— to know that Congress placed libraries into that category. Also included in that are museums, galleries, things of that nature. Establishments providing services are a very large category: dry cleaners, banks, offices of health care providers, offices of doctors, accountants, funeral parlors, things of that nature.

Places of recreation include parks, zoos, amusement parks, stations used for public transit. Establishments providing social services range from day-care centers to senior citizens' centers. Again, a very broad category covered by Title 3. Places of exercise are gyms, health clubs, golf courses, for those of you who golf. My friends in wheelchairs don't want us to find an answer to exactly what an accessible sand trap is. Places of education and places of public gathering include convention centers, lecture halls, things of that nature.

For those of you who are not with libraries, but maybe associations, it's important to keep in mind the definition of public accommodation is an entity that leases or leases to one of these types of entities. If you rent hotel space, you can be covered by the ADA for the purposes of the convention, meeting, or conference, and you have full ADA obligations.

The ADA also covers, in addition to those very broad categories, something called *commercial facilities,* which means office buildings, warehouses, things of that nature.

I will mention two exceptions. One is that religious organizations or entities controlled by religious organizations are not covered by the ADA. If you are in a library that is controlled by a church group, you are totally exempt from Title 3 of the ADA. I don't know if that happens with libraries; it happens with day-care and senior centers. Private clubs are exempt under Title 3 to the extent that they are a private club. If the local Elks hall opens itself up to the public, it becomes a public accommodation, but if it keeps services for persons that are part of the private club, they are exempt from the ADA.

The range of obligations for public accommodations go beyond new construction and alterations. Auxiliary aids are clearly included. In addition, there is a range of other kinds of obligations, the most immediate of which may be the obligation to review your policies, practices, and procedures and to make modifications in those policies, practices, and procedures where it is necessary to provide services to persons with disabilities. You have this obligation. Again, there is a limit under its fundamental alteration program.

A requirement that no pets can come into your library must be modified to allow someone with a Seeing Eye dog. It's a very simple concept, but it's one that will play itself out in a number of ways.

If you have a policy that says you do not provide assistance to people in terms of going into the shelves and getting books for them or helping them with the card catalog, you may have to modify that policy for persons with disabilities. You might not have to if you are a one-person operation. That would be considered a fundamental alteration.

One of the strengths of the ADA and one of the reasons it's been successful today is it's a fair and balanced statute. There is a requirement to modify existing policies and practices. There is a realization there has to be a limit—only if it's reasonable and only if it doesn't fundamentally alter your program.

If an auxiliary is going to cost too much, and it may, especially for smaller entities, there is a limitation on that. And there is a balance. This balance, I think, provides flexibility; a lot of people like to look at it as vagueness. I suppose there are two sides to the same coin. I think it's important, and I think you can use it to your advantage. The idea is that this law should be a flexible one, one that allows you to make your program successful to persons with disabilities. It applies to libraries that are small, community libraries with no budget that just exist with volunteer help, to a big library with a large but shrinking budget in a major metropolitan area.

The law applies to those situations, and it has been written in a way so that it can apply. It will provide accessibility but do so in a means available to you.

Finally in this primer, it is a civil rights law. Let's look at how it is enforced. One thing Congress wanted to do with the ADA was empower persons with disabilities. The ADA gives to persons with disabilities the ability to go into court, to federal district court, if they are parties.

So under Title 1, Title 2, and Title 3, individuals with disabilities have access to courts through bringing their own lawsuit. There is also a role of the federal government here. Under Title 1, complaints must be filed with the EEOC, and Title 1 is enforced much the same way as Title 7 of the Civil Rights Act of 1974. For those of you familiar with Title 7, this is very much the same. The person files a complaint with the EEOC, which will either investigate or give the person a "right to sue" letter.

Under Title 1, a person can get injunctive relief if you have built your building in an inaccessible fashion. They can get a court order requiring the building to be altered. If they prevail, they can get reasonable attorneys' fees, and because of the civil rights law that was signed not too long ago by President Bush, in cases of intentional discrimination, persons with disabilities can get monetary damages if they, for example, suffer pain and humiliation. There is a cap on what it is. It depends on the size of the covered entity in terms of how much they can get in that kind of situation. When you are dealing with that kind of situation, you are usually talking about a jury trial. If someone is seeking injunctive relief, you are talking about a trial by a judge.

With Title 2, an individual can go right into court, or they can file a complaint with one of eight designated federal agencies. What we have done is divide up responsibility for investigating complaints among eight federal agencies. The Department of Justice has oversight responsibility to make sure it works.

The Department of Education has been designated as the agency to take complaints regarding libraries. If someone is going to complain about a library that's covered by Title 2, that complaint will be handled by the Department of Education, by the Office of Civil Rights.

Under Title 2, again, if a person or the federal

government goes into court, we can get injunctive relief. If a person goes into court they can get attorneys' fees if they prevail. If you are sued and it was a frivolous suit and you prevail, and the court decides it was frivolous, you can get attorneys' fees from the person who sued.

There is some doubt about compensatory damages under Title 2. Not too long ago only the Ninth Circuit, which is the circuit in the San Francisco area, West Coast circuit, allowed for compensatory damages under Section 504. Since Section 504 is the model for Title 2 in the Ninth Circuit, there are probably compensatory damages.

This year the Supreme Court, in a case dealing with sexual harassment (this was the first time this issue was in the Supreme Court), said under Title 9 of the amendment of 1972, which is a parallel civil rights statute, that a woman who was discriminated against can get compensatory damages for pain and suffering and humiliation. It was a very strong case. Because the language is the same as 504, the same as Title 2, it is at least likely that courts will find that persons that are intentionally discriminated against under Title 2 may also be able to get compensatory damages. I think we will have to wait and see what happens as cases develop.

Finally, under Title 3, if individuals sue, they cannot get compensatory damages; they can only get injunctive relief. If the Department of Justice brings a suit, we can't get compensatory damages for a particular suit, but we can get civil penalties of up to $50,000 for the first violation and up to $100,000 for a future violation. That's a legalism in the statute. The statute also requires the federal government to provide technical assistance. By that, the statute means providing information to entities that are covered by the ADA as to what their responsibilities are, and providing information to people who are protected by the ADA to let them know what their rights are. It is very much our view that we are not seeking to see how many lawsuits are going to pile up. Our job is to let people know about the ADA and worry about compliance.

Thus far, our theory is first we educate, then we negotiate, and only after that do we litigate. I think I can tell you the response to the ADA has been very positive. We are in our infancy, but there has been a great willingness to cooperate. I'm particularly pleased with the private sector. We have gotten a very strong response from those entities that are in the business of providing services to people. There is some concern, obviously, confusion about exactly what they have to do, when it kicks in, and how it works. There is a willingness to comply. That's not uniform; there are problem areas.

I think state and local governments have probably been more reticent to comply than the private sector, I think that's because they may be feeling the financial pinch of the recession a little more strongly, and there are some difficulties.

The impact of the law is very clear. We have received a number of complaints; we have gotten about 250 in Title 3 and another 200 in Title 2. Most have been barrier-removal kinds of issues. Frankly, many have dealt with doctor's offices. There seems to be a large population that is creating problems in the ADA world. I don't know of many that involve library issues. I think the initial response we have seen from libraries is a positive one.

You have a definite role to play. In my own community, the library is much more than a place, a place of public display. On Capitol Hill in Washington, D.C., our local library is really a focal point for our community. We go there to hear lectures, we go there for poetry readings, we go there for community meetings. My local branch librarian knows my reading tastes, strange as they may be. He knows my wife's. If there is something that he comes across, he will suggest it to us as something we might be interested in. It's a very important part of what makes life worthwhile in our community.

I think what the ADA is saying is that these kinds of services, these kinds of opportunities should now be open to persons with disabilities. It's certainly a challenge. There are expenses involved, but I think it's a very worthwhile, legitimate role for the government to play.

I think that this preconference is a good one because we are at the beginning. We are learning what it is that we have to do and how to go about doing it. I hope that we will be able to answer some of your questions and get information to you because we really are viewed with our goal of taking what is in fact a piece of paper, the law, and making it a reality. I think it will be a difficult and challenging job, but it's one that really is at the heart of what we, as a form of government and a democratic country, are all about.

I wish you luck in your activities in the remainder of the year.

A Historical Overview

Mary Lou Breslin

I want to take just a moment to thank the association for the opportunity to discuss the ADA. I will address the act from a consumer perspective. First, I will examine the ADA from the perspective, not of a person with a disability necessarily, but from a historical perspective. The opportunity to talk about the origins of ADA will help us to understand where the legislation came from, why it's important, and why the provisions, and I will be touching on making the ADA a reality.

I think that for many of us the ADA may seem to have appeared from Jupiter or Mars, and very quickly. I want to assure you that the ADA is both a process and a product of a long struggle in the disabilities civil rights movement. It has been evolving in interesting and important ways over a period of twenty years. I want to touch on some of the historic events that led to the passage of the ADA.

I also just want to say, too, that it's really a unique opportunity to talk with librarians. I was thinking about what you all do in your work day-to-day. You have a lot of interesting roles with respect to ADA. I think what motivated most of you to attend this preconference is the fact that your entities, whether public or private libraries, have an obligation to comply with the law. The ADA requires that your employment practices, your programs, and your facilities be made accessible to people with disabilities. That is your primary concern. You also have several other roles. I want to appeal to these other roles in the course of my remarks this morning.

In addition to the requirement to comply with the law yourselves, you have a responsibility as public educators. You are being asked for materials, documentation, and resources that are available. As librarians, you especially will be positioned to educate about the ADA. One of your functions is to make this information available to the public.

So not only are you looking at the ADA because you are required to comply with it, but you are also looking at the ADA as a subject in which the public is interested.

Finally, I think each and every one of you is committed to some extent to promoting information about the past, about history. I want to appeal to you to learn a little bit about the history of the disability rights movement to help you in your educational role.

It's important for you as historians within the library context to know about the history of this political movement. The disability rights movement is an important social movement that is responsible for the ADA. I hope my remarks will enable you to go back to your communities with a fuller understanding of where the ADA came from and what your roles and responsibilities are when you get home, in addition to worrying about whether or not you have to put your books in braille.

I have a personal perspective that might be a little helpful to us in the course of working

---

Mary Lou Breslin is Senior Policy Advisor at the Disability Rights Education and Defense Fund in Berkeley, California.

together now and in the future. That perspective springs from a couple of sources.

The first is that I am a person with a disability—I use a wheelchair, as you can see. Second, I also have been associated with a national law and policy center Disability Rights Education Defense Fund, DREDF, since it was founded in the late 1970s. DREDF is dedicated to promoting civil rights for people with disabilities, which has been its core mission since the organization was founded in 1979.

This dual perspective is a perspective that has helped, I think, to shape the ADA, not so much with respect to my contribution, but with respect to the contribution of people with disabilities around the country.

I want to talk about the origins of the ADA. Let's first look at what kind of social policy models we have had in place in this country to deal with people with disabilities. What's important about these models is that they have undergone incredible changes over the last twenty years. If you leave with nothing else, I hope you have an appreciation for the enormous progress we have made in terms of the way we view people with disabilities and the issues people with disabilities face.

Before 1970, we had a social policy model based on the provision of rehabilitative or medical services. After the passage of the key federal civil rights legislation, Section 504 of the 1973 Rehabilitation Act, we have a model based on an entirely different principle. This new model is based on a civil rights perspective. Let me tell you about what I think the differences between the models are, and stories that illustrate these points.

Before the 1970s, we had a model that was predicated on the idea that if you have a disability, the burden of dealing with the consequences of disability rests on you the individual. There was no larger societal responsibility for dealing with the burden of those consequences. In order to illustrate that point, let me tell you a quick story.

I became disabled as a kid. I was living in Louisville, Kentucky, at that time. When I got polio, as happened in those days, I had been going to a private Catholic school. I took about four months off to go through a rehabilitation program. When it was time to go back to school, my family was confronted with what was really a major dilemma. They had to decide what steps to take so I could continue my education.

They would probably deny this, if they had to think about it, but in retrospect they were really effective advocates. They took the position that I was the same kid after I began to use a wheelchair as I was before I used the wheelchair. There was no reason from their perspective that I ought not to be in school with kids my own age, participating in all the same kinds of activities in which eleven or twelve year olds participate.

They could see no reason why I ought not to be able to continue in regular school. The problem was I had been going to the girl's Catholic school, which had stone steps up to the classrooms in all the buildings. There were a number of such buildings on the campus, so that school was really not a possibility. This was certainly an architectural barrier problem, but it presented itself as a much larger social policy problem.

So my family began to look around for possible alternatives. They approached the local school district, who said they had a program for "crippled children." It's called the School for Crippled Children. It was a residential program. They would have been happy to take me. I would have been welcome there, and I would have been taken care of there.

The skeptical expression on my father's face remains vividly in my mind today. He knew there was something wrong with this picture, but he wasn't sure what it was. Intuitively, he knew sending me to the school for crippled children wasn't the right thing to do. My parents shopped around and discovered it was really going to be a difficult problem to solve, mainly because most of the public schools were architecturally inaccessible.

Finally, they did locate a public school, which had been recently built. It had three stories, with one step into the ground floor level but no elevator to the second or third floor. They thought that because I could get into the first floor, it was worth considering. Remember that my mother weedled the principal into allowing me to be admitted by basically saying that I didn't need any help or anything special. So let's just try it.

I remember very vividly my first day of classes. I went to my home room, which in fact was on the first floor. I was given a class card. The class card tells you where your classes are throughout the day.

I looked at my class card. It was clear I had a problem. I had biology on the third floor and civics on the first floor and English back on the third floor. I went to my home room teacher, whose eyebrows went up. She got the principal. The three of us huddled in the hallway to try to figure out what to do about the problem.

The only thing that anybody could come up with was that the four biggest boys in school would be assigned the responsibility of carrying me up and down the stairs to my classes during the day.

Remember back to your high school days? Do you remember the stack of books that you carted around with you all day? Well I would leave class five minutes early, go out to the stairs, and these guys would stack their books on my lap. I would peer over the top of the books. I was younger, thinner, and using a manual wheelchair, so it was not as impossible as it might appear today.

Each person would position themselves on a corner of my wheelchair. No, they wouldn't tip it back, taking the chair up or down a step at a time. I would be lifted up off the ground and they would run as fast as they could up and down the stairs. Indeed every day, six or seven times a day, we ran up and down the steps, while I peered over the top of the books.

It was an interesting time. I never was dropped and nobody, I think, was injured in the course of carrying me. It was an unusual time because I was the only kid in school with a visible disability. There probably were kids with disabilities that they managed to hide from everybody. I was the only kid that had a noticeable disability.

For those of you who have disabilities and are my age, you will not find this to be a unique story. I tell it to you because it really makes several points about the need for a shift in the social policy model that eventually led to the ADA.

One of the important points is that none of us, including myself, my family, the principal, my teachers, or the kids who carried me up and down the stairs, ever thought that it would make sense to move the English class from the third floor to the first floor rather than carrying me up and down the stairs to those classes every day.

Also, there was no wheelchair-accessible bathroom in my school. In those days there wasn't a door wide enough to get my wheelchair through in order to reach the toilet. The simple solution would have been to remove the bathroom door and hang a curtain; it might have cost $10 to solve the problem. We didn't discuss it, we didn't ask for it. We didn't raise the question.

Therefore, I was unable to use the bathroom for three and a half years during school due to the lack of a wheelchair-accessible bathroom.

It was okay to have a disability in those days, if you could camouflage your disability—both in a psychological as well as physical sense. If you needed some method to level the playing field, such as architectural access or programmatic access in some form or the kind of technology that we see here today, you didn't have a chance because it pointed to your differences from the mainstream of nondisabled people.

I think the major philosophical shift over the past twenty years has been away from the social policy model built on the idea that rehabilitative and medical services and care are intended to make one as able-bodied as possible. Then, equipped with near–able-bodiedness, you would go out and deal with the world as it was— inaccessible with architectural and attitudinal barriers.

Many of us with disabilities believed in this model. I bought into it personally because it was a part of what we all believed at the time. The tenents of the model were very pervasive. It took many years to move the process along to change that model. My experience is only intended to point out to you that this model was destructive in a lot of ways.

I want to talk a little bit about the last several decades, which have led to the passage of the landmark ADA. I want to establish a few landmarks for you to keep in mind as you are asking questions about ADA.

In the late 1960s, the federal government began to be somewhat responsive to complaints that federal buildings did not provide architectural access to people with disabilities. There is some logic here. You pay taxes, so you ought to be able to get into federal institutions where you vote, get your marriage licenses and passports, go to court, and undertake the activities of a citizen. If you had a disability, a physical disability in particular, these buildings were inaccessible.

There was a major move in the mid-1960s for federal facilities to voluntarily make themselves accessible. Of course after a period of three or four years, there had been almost no voluntary attempt by federal entities to go forward with some architectural barrier removal within their own facilities. This necessitated the passage of the first disability rights law. The Architectural Barriers Act of 1968 required the access to federal facilities. It was really the beginning of the political movement of people with disabilities. By passing the 1968 law, Congress recognized that volunteerism wasn't going to work in this area. Congress needed to take appropriate steps to mandate certain kinds of actions by federal agencies to remove barriers. This was an important step. In the early

1970s, we saw one of the most important events in the political process leading to the ADA. This was the enactment of Section 504 of the 1973 Rehabilitation Act.

Those of you who are familiar with 504 will realize it has been the model for the ADA. For the first time, Section 504 barred discriminations against people with disabilities in federally funded programs. Section 504 was modeled after the 1964 Civil Rights Act, which banned discrimination against racial minorities and women.

Its enactment was incredibly important because, for the first time, Congress recognized discrimination as the root cause of isolation and segregation of people with disabilities. Section 504 also acknowledged that people with disabilities belong to a class, regardless of the type of disability, whose members experience the same root causes of isolation and exclusion.

With the enactment of 504, we have shifted from charity and rehabilitation-based policy to what we think of as a sociopolitical policy model. This is the beginning of a two-decade process to further enhance the civil rights of people with disabilitites, culminating in the passage of the ADA. This nearly twenty-year process has been a remarkable one because the shift from a rehab-charity orientation to disability policy to a sociopolitical orientation is both historic and unique in this country and in the world. The passage of the ADA represents a dramatic shift from out-of-sight-out-of-mind to a civil rights model built on the twin goals of equal treatment and integration.

With disability, there are several interesting differences that distinguish civil rights issues in the work environment and in community programs from those of minorities or women. Let me tell you a few quick stories about how this plays out.

After Section 504 was enacted in 1973, and before regulations were issued by the Department of Health, Education and Welfare in 1971, several things happened. We had a law that says you can't discriminate against disabled people in federally funded programs, but no one had any idea what that meant. No one knew what discrimination meant in the area of disability. After the law was enacted and the regulations were published, some key concepts were defined. These key concepts are central, I think, to the ADA.

Let me tell you about several court cases that are interesting and that have to do with the evolution of these key concepts. These are both federal court cases that had to do with transit issues. Those of you who have been following the various debates about the disability community, which has been pressing for accessible public transit, will find these interesting.

Both of these cases had to do with individuals who used wheelchairs. Both had to do with attempts by these individuals to board public buses. In both instances, it was impossible to board the buses because the buses were not lift equipped. Both cases went through the federal court system.

Let me tell you what the two different rulings were regarding the same problems.

In one case, the judge looked at the case and applied a traditional civil rights approach. The idea is, if the driver opens the door, looks out to the person with a disability using a wheelchair and says come in, you are welcome to come in. He or she is not preventing the passenger from coming in, based on disability.

Essentially the message was, if you could get out of your wheelchair and throw it up on the bus and crawl up the stairs and then get back in your wheelchair, then no discrimination had occurred.

In the other case, the judge had a different approach to the solution. He looked at the facts of situation and said well, if you are sitting out there on the sidewalk in your wheelchair and there are steps on the bus, those steps represent a barrier. Those steps are what in fact constitute the means by which the person with a disability is discriminated against. So the transit district must take some affirmative steps to, in this case, remove the stairs to the bus to enable the person to board. His definition of what nondiscrimination on the basis of disability meant was to rule that these affirmative steps needed to be taken.

These two cases are really important because they highlight what you are dealing with in your local library situations as you begin to think about implementation of ADA.

It is necessary to balance the rights of people with disabilities with the cost and burden, both administrative and financial, to society to level the playing field to assure equal opportunity for people with disabilities. These two cases illustrate the balancing act that went on when the ADA was drafted, and the disability rights community recognizes that it is necessary to make certain compromises in order to advance the concept of disability as a legitimate civil rights issue.

The result of this process was that limits were set, and the concept of limits being set in disability rights law is very important. There are several ways in which limits get set—for example, the concept of program access in Title 2.

Program access is a compromise. Program access recognizes that existing buildings have architectural barriers, that it might be costly to remove them, but that those buildings house programs that people need to get to. So the compromise is to move those programs or in some other way make them accessible rather than requiring a retrofit of every existing building, although a retrofit will sometimes be the only solution to provide access.

So the disability community recognized that it was important to set the tone, to accept that certain limits needed to be set to further the goal of integration and equal participation.

The disability community recognized, too, that in new construction of physical buildings, there was very little excuse not to provide architectural access. This is what we call the look-to-the-future provision. It recognizes that I might not live long enough to see full architectural access in the society as a whole, but my kids and grandkids are going to benefit from this plan to provide access, not barriers, when buildings are constrtucted.

In the employment area, there are also principles from Section 504 that are used by the ADA that use the concept of setting limits. They are the concepts of reasonable accommodation and undue hardship in employment.

We know from personal experience and from research that myth and stereotype about disability result in exclusion of people with disabilities from the workplace. Some instances in accomodation may be needed so a person with a disability can work. The right of a disabled person to receive reasonable accomodations is balanced against the right of the employer to not have an unnecessary burden imposed on him or her. This principle became an accepted practice as Section 504 was implemented and consequently was carried forward to the ADA. So we have this process of setting limits and of establishing basic principles that the disability rights movement as a whole has been working for.

I would like to spend a moment, if I might, to discuss what has gone on in the courts in addition to the two transit examples that I have just discussed. In almost no other place do we see such a transformation as in the way the U.S. Supreme Court views disability rights issues compared to a decade ago. It's an interesting and I think a very enlightening process that we have seen in the last ten years or so. The Court has become educated through the same process Congress was educated about the need for the ADA. Society, as a consequence, is going to change its view of disability.

In the late 1970s, a case was heard by the U.S. Supreme Court involving a woman with a hearing disability who applied to nursing school. This is known as the Davis case. She was denied admission because the school believed that she wouldn't be able to train as a nurse because of her hearing disability. This was the first very important disability rights case that was heard by the Court. The opinion of the Court in this case represented the attitudes of society as a whole about disability.

The disability community had recognized the need for a policy to level the playing field. The idea of accommodation and affirmative steps to enable a person with a disability to board the bus had become a fundamental principle.

The case involving the woman with a hearing disability is very interesting because the Supreme Court hadn't gotten that message yet. The Court was still applying the pre-1970s charity and rehabilitative social policy model to disability. The Court found that the woman with a hearing disability was not qualified to participate in the nursing program.

Let me share with you a quote from the decision in that case. The Court said "technological advances can be expected to advance opportunities to rehabilitate the handicapped or otherwise qualify them for some useful employment."

From a disability rights perspective, this is an unsatisfactory interpretation of Section 504. The decision didn't take into the account the fact that provision of an accommodation could equalize the opportunity and participation.

These are really important concepts because the Court used an analysis that most of the disability community had rejected for a decade. The Court simply had not yet been educated about the new civil rights social policy model.

I'm going to mention some events that occurred during the 1980s because they are also central to the successful passage of the ADA. The disability community was beginning to gain clout and political power during the 1980s. People with disabilities began taking control over programs and over the direction of social policy. These events really became central to enforcing the civil rights laws enacted in the 1970s and working towards passage of the ADA.

In the early 1980s, there was an attempt to deregulate Section 504. The efforts by the disability community to put the Section 504 regulations in place were very important in disability rights history. People with disabilities occupied federal buildings and lobbied aggressively to get these regulations promulgated because they interpreted and defined 504.

Once those regulations were in place, they embodied those basic principles I mentioned previously. No sooner had they been put in place when there was an attempt by the Reagan administration to weaken them.

This attempt was based on the belief that people with disabilities weren't going to be powerful enough to object. If it was possible to deregulate disability rights laws, it was probably possible to undercut other civil rights laws. It was clear at the time that a strategic error had been made by the administration.

One of the important victories in the early 1980s was that people with disabilities were able to prevent deregulation through an organized effort lobbying elected representatives and working behind the scenes to be able to influence the process. As a result almost forty thousand letters from people with disabilities arrived at the White House when the administration thought that people wouldn't even notice these regulations were being done away with.

The process of saving the 504 regulations in the early 1980s is pivotal because these regulations had been crafted to include the key principles I just mentioned. These concepts have all been tested and brought forward, and are now incorporated within the ADA.

So in each step along the way we have seen social policy change because of intervention of the disability community. We have seen the building blocks begin to line up that will lead us to the ADA.

As a means of comparison, I want to draw your attention next to another U.S. Supreme Court case. This is a case that was decided in the late 1980s involving a woman who had been a teacher in Florida and who had tuberculosis. As a result of her condition, she was not allowed to return to her classroom by a school district in Florida. This case is interesting and important in the progression of the disability rights movement and from an historical perspective.

Do you remember our discussion about the fact that the Court did not understand the application of the concept of accommodation in the Davis case? Well, in the case involving the woman who had tuberculosis, the Court adopted the civil rights perspective that the disability community had been promoting. It did so because the Court had been educated over a period of time by considering other disability cases, with input from organizations representing people with disabilities around the country who were committed to shaping the Court's attitude toward disability.

Let me just remind you of the quote I read to you from the Davis case. I would like you to compare it to the case involving the woman who had tuberculosis. "Congress acknowledged that society's accumulated myths and fears about disability and diseases are as handicapping as are the physical limitations that flow from actual impairments."

You see the progression of the Court's attitude toward people with disabilities? You see the Court's recognition of the shift from the old social policy model of rehabilitation and charity to the new sociopolitical model? This is an important shift because the ADA drew upon this case to develop legislative history to the law itself. The decision helped the drafters of the ADA to think conceptually about the purpose of the ADA. So I hope you can see that this progression is historically important and represents the successes the movement attained.

One other important thing that happened in the mid-1980s that led to the success of the ADA is that the disability rights community managed to elevate disability as a legitimate civil rights cause within the civil rights community itself. The community became very involved in the broader coalition of organizations promoting civil rights. This participation enabled the disability community to marshal support for the ADA by the broader civil rights community.

There is a national organization, The Leadership Conference on Civil Rights, which has been working for decades to promote civil rights for many disenfranchised groups. It took on the ADA as its primary purpose and goal in the late 1980s. That's important because twenty years earlier there had been an attempt to amend the 1964 Civil Rights Act to include people with disabilities, which had failed because there was no recognition that disability was a legitimate civil rights issue. So as you can see, we have come a long way.

History is important in a sense that we made enormous strides in a very short period of time. We made inroads into a community that did not recognize our issues heretofore in terms of policy making at the highest level of the land. The result really is passage.

In conclusion, let me summarize some of the

themes that I think have emerged over the last few of decades. One of the most important themes is that of equity.

Equity really became the moral force behind the ADA. This is true with respect to the goals of other civil rights movements and it's true with respect to goals of the disability rights movements and the ADA.

The second theme is the one that brought us here. It's the reason you are here with questions because you know that implementation of the ADA depends upon your ability to take this information, work with it in your community, work with it in your facilities, and educate the public that comes in to ask you questions as well.

Finally, the ADA was necessary, despite enormous gains in the civil rights community, for a couple of reasons. Many of you are probably familiar with the statistics that became very much used in the process of seeing the ADA come to fruition. A couple of them need to be reiterated because they are fairly astonishing, I think.

There are forty-three million people with disabilities in the United States. That's an astonishing number, if you think about it. I have been asked how many people with disabilities would take advantage of an accessible hotel. We don't know how many people will take advantage of an accessible hotel, but we do know that potentially all forty-three million people could benefit from this statute.

We have learned from a poll that was done by the Lou Harris organization in the mid-1980s that nearly two-thirds of working-age people working with disabilities are unemployed or severely underemployed. That's an astonishing and very depressing figure.

It was clear that the victories of the disability rights movement with respect to federal Civil Rights laws and legitimizing disability as a civil rights issue had not had the effect on people on the street and in the community that we had hoped they would have.

The two statistics I just mentioned are important for you to keep in mind if you question why the ADA has the kind of requirements it does when you may not have seen people with disabilities in your programs, when you don't see many people in your community who have disabilities, or when you are not familiar with the extent of disability among the people you serve and with whom you work. People with disabilities are in your communities. Barriers and attitudes have kept them isolated and segregated for too long. Those statistics need to be kept in mind as we work toward compliance.

Last, I think it's important to remember that attitudes about disability are very deeply ingrained, that you may not know how deeply seated they are.

I want to close by telling you a great story about something that happened to me a couple years ago that I think illustrates the point about how our attitudes are so much controlled by both what we have learned as kids and young adults and also by what we see as the disability issues in our community.

I was in New York a few years ago on a mission with the Ford Foundation in an attempt to generate some income for my organization. We had been doing civil rights work for some time and we thought the Ford Foundation would be an appropriate place to get support for basic civil rights. We had spent six months in meetings and had asked Itzhak Perlman, the world-reknowned violinist, to join us.

We were going to make our best pitch for support. We had prepared, we were very excited about the possibilities of meeting the vice-president of the foundation, and we were actually about to move out of our hotel and go to the meeting. As it happened, I was meeting a colleague in Grand Central Station, and I was heading to the elevator from above ground. I had gone down to the station, and I was going to be meeting a couple of people. One or two people would be joining me to go to this meeting.

I had stopped to get myself a cup of coffee and was holding my cup while waiting for the person I was meeting. I had my briefcase and I was ready to go to a professional meeting. I was sitting in Grand Central Station watching the terminal where my colleague and I had agreed to meet, holding my coffee cup, when a very well dressed, middle-aged woman walked by and dropped a quarter in my coffee cup. I was so stunned and shocked. First of all, that wasn't enough money to replace the coffee. And it was the only money I made on that trip.

I tell you this story because it's very important to look within yourselves as you think about your attitudes toward people with disabilities. Don't make assumptions that may or may not be grounded in fact.

I think that those very kinds of unquestioning attitudes have been at the heart of exclusion of people with disabilities in this country, and I think if we can recognize these issues we can be more effective in making the ADA a reality.

JOHNSON: Another landmark piece of legislation that you see in the ADA is PL 94142, which passed in 1972 and was then called the Education of all Handicapped Children's Act. Two principles of PL 94142 are present in the ADA.

One is the principle of integration and placing persons with disabilities in the least restrictive environment. The second is the individualization of decisions regarding reasonable accommodation or employment as it relates to persons with disabilities.

The presentation was an excellent one in terms of getting that history, of seeing where the ADA came from 94142 was pivotal as well in the building blocks of the principles and themes that we see in the ADA.

An Administrator's View of "What Is Doable"

Joseph Shubert

What I'm going to discuss is the responsibility and the perspective of the library administrator for services to all people within the community. Every library has a community library, whether it's a school library, academic library, special library, public library, institution. Each of us who is responsible for a library has a community we are supposed to be serving. We are all acutely aware there are people in our community who use us enthusiastically, a lot, and there are a lot of people who are not using our libraries. That prompts, or should prompt, a series of questions for us here.

Questions are important to administrators of any type of a library. I'm going to start with some figures about the nation as a whole because this year 164 million people will use public libraries. They will borrow 1.4 billion books and other materials, and they will ask, and get answers to some 201 million reference questions. These users come from almost every sector of American society.

We know that many of the forty-three million Americans with disabilities are among these library users and that many are not.

If asked their reasons for not using public libraries, like many other Americans, those with disabilities might respond that they don't have sufficient time to use library services, that they feel they have no need for library services, that they find our library hours inconvenient, that they are not sure what the library has to offer them, that they believe the library is too far away to use conveniently, or that they find the library or major parts of it inaccessible to them.

We don't know how many Americans with disabilities did not use their public libraries because they couldn't get through the doors last year or get to the materials they needed, because they couldn't communicate by phone or in person because of one or more disabilities, or because they don't know what the library has to offer.

If they knew what the library had to offer, many would want information that they might get most easily by talking to a reference librarian by phone. Others would want to sit and talk with a librarian about books and reading or attend a library program. The techies would like to get information from the libraries with their home computer and others would want their children in a summer reading program.

In short, the expectations of Americans with disabilities are not unlike those of other library users.

Why Should We Be Concerned?

At the White House conference almost a year ago, delegates urged the marketing of public library services as a means of serving more

---

Joseph Shubert is New York State Librarian and Assistant Commissioner for Libraries, Albany. The author appreciates the suggestions and assistance given by the following people during the course of preparing this paper: Roberta Cade, Sara Dallas, Carol Ann Desch, Glyn T. Evans, Laura Flynn, Carole Huxley, Rita Levay, Judith Levine, Dahlia Mazengia, Carol Sheffer, Jane Somers, GladysAnn Wells, and Jerome Yavarkovsky.

people and securing more advocates for library support. I'm going to suggest three important reasons why we must be concerned about marketing services to people with disabilities.

First of all, they are part of the community we are committed to serve, and we have an opportunity to serve more people within our community. Second, we are a service organization; we care about people. And third, it's the law.

In preparing this paper, I worked with several assumptions: each of us wants to serve more people, our resources for services are limited, and we are willing to set a priority for library service to the entire community, including people with disabilities.

The changes the ADA seeks to bring about depend upon our involving ourselves—directors, library staffs, trustees in the community—in assessing, planning, and providing library services to the entire community, institution, or school.

Each library, public school, university, or community college serves a community in which there are people with disabilities. It may help us to remember that we all live our lives between the incapacity of infancy and potential disability. Some of us simply enjoy longer periods of time between those two points. While one in six persons is born with a disability, some five hundred thousand other people become disabled each year.[1]

Every day, a thousand Americans pass the age of sixty-five. As we pass that milestone, we come closer to a period of time, shorter or longer, of some kind of permanent disability. So whatever responsibilities you and I hold in the library or wherever we are in our lifetime, this act relates to us.

Where Do We Start?

To implement the ADA, as in any question of priority of library service, the first step is to review our policies and our priorities. What in your library's mission statement and policy are you on record as saying about service and access to all members of the community? Does that statement need to include language about clients with special needs, and what, if anything, needs to be added to that policy statement?

The initiative can begin with the director, but as the diversity of participants in this conference suggests, it can come from anyone. Total quality management tells us the person who has the concern must promptly start working with others, but, for the moment, let's start with that one person who is willing to ask those questions about policy, community, and users.

Many years ago at a Nevada Library Association conference, Edwin Castagna gave simple advice to library directors.

> Make it a point at least once a month to walk through the front door of your library and try to look at it at the way the first-time visitor would see it. Give everything in sight a "first time" look.

Over the years, I found his advice sound. That kind of walkabout can lead to a cleaner, more inviting library and lead to the changes that make the library easier to use.

As we take Castagna's advice, we should take the walkabout in the company of a couple of library users with disabilities. We should learn the problems that they may experience with doors, steps, circulation desks, library catalogs, index tables, placement of terminals, and drinking fountains, all of which we find perfectly convenient for us.

Who Else Needs to Get Involved?

If you take these first two steps—thinking about policy and taking the walkabout—the next important question is, Who else needs to be involved? Modifying services, making changes, and reaching out to new users is not done casually. It requires the insight, knowledge, and creativity of staff, trustees, users, and people particularly concerned with services to particular segments of the community. Implementing the services and changes expected by ADA must involve the entire organization because it will affect the entire organization.

At the Mohawk Valley Library Association in Schenectady, New York, it was discovered more than ten years ago that various groups and centers that serve special populations are knowledgeable and willing to help improve library service and access for everyone.

MVLA, Mohawk Valley Library Association, is a cooperative library system with fourteen member libraries serving communities ranging in size from about 1,000 to 150,000. A third of the member libraries serve communities with populations smaller than 2,500.

When that system and its member libraries set out ten years ago to develop coordinated services, they cooperated with two neighboring systems that were developing similar programs.[2] Each of the three systems organized an advisory committee. MVLA sought committee members from various organizations, including the Capitol District Center for Independent Living.

The center, as its name suggests, recognizes that people with disabilities are consumers of services and that they can direct services that they use. The center helps people build skills, gain self-confidence, explore opportunities, make decisions, and assert their rights. In short, it helps people become more independent by assuming control over their own lives.

The center staff works with people with disabilities and with their families. They also work with community organizations and leaders to break down physical and attitudinal barriers that stand in the way of independence.

One of the center staff members, Larry Lazarek, was the deaf services coordinator, and he became a member of the MVLA advisory committee. He helped the committee and the MVLA staff and library staffs understand disabilities, develop services, and take advantage of contacts and services of the center and those of other organizations. One specific result of his involvement was that MVLA libraries were among the first in New York State to use the New York telephone relay services for library users who are deaf.

Well, that happened ten years ago. What is MVLA doing now? People with disabilities are a part of the total library service community, and as MVLA carries out its LSCA Title I Senior Citizens Outreach Program, a number of libraries service people with disabilities right up front. Libraries and branches that are physically accessible (about 80 percent of the libraries in the system) are listed in the electronic database that the Center for Independent Living now operates. The database was started by a woman architect, and it includes information about more than physical access.

This year, MVLA conducted workshops at three member libraries. Fonda has a population of about one thousand and serves an area of about three thousand people. Schenectady serves a county of 150,000 people and is central library for three other counties. Mary Nicolau, the director, and Sarah Dallas, the services coordinator, point out that the library system's connections with organizations provide member libraries with materials, insights, and expertise that enable them to reach new users.

What Do Involved People Do?

At the New York State Library, we took a different tack in extending services to individuals with disabilities. The State Library is one of three major institutions in the New York State Office of Cultural Education, which in turn is a part of the State Education Department. The State Library is a research library with a collection of more than two million volumes, and in addition to its research library services, it functions as a regional library, serving some twenty-five thousand readers with talking books, braille, and other special materials. In the words of the governor who established the library in 1818, it is "a public library for the government and the people of the state."

We have about 365,000 square feet in the Cultural Education Center. The center is a 1.3 million-square-foot building designed by the architects of Lincoln Center and completed in 1978. As you are well aware, most buildings constructed in the 1970s were not designed for the needs of people with disabilities in mind. So we, the state museum and the archives, which are located in that center, shared a common concern about this over the years and had attempted to reduce the barriers.

In 1990, our deputy commissioner for cultural education committed to a comprehensive staff-wide program to ensure that individuals with disabilities have access to library, museum, and archive services and programs. The first thing the deputy commissioner did was appoint her assistant to lead an access subcommittee of fifteen staff members from the library, the archives, the museum, and public broadcasting and staff from the Office of Vocational and Education Services for Individuals with Disabilities. Over sixteen months, that group developed a detailed plan for the specific priorities for:

- the safety of all persons within the building,
- employment opportunity,
- the use of public broadcasts to expand awareness of disabilities and access, and
- leadership for expanded access in libraries, museums, historical societies, and other cultural institutions with which we work throughout the state.

Committee members coordinated their plans in a department-wide planning council, but, most important, they used focus groups, brainstorming sessions, and a variety of other means to get the ideas and awareness of all the five hundred people who work in the institutions and those of people with disabilities who want to use those services. The subcommittee's work did not end with the approval of a plan. A plan produces change only if it's used and if the results are tracked. Our plan includes a firm commitment for regular evaluation and updating.

In the first twelve-month evaluation session we had a few weeks ago, we identified six areas in which we achieved significant progress: employment, physical access, publications, finding guides, awareness, and staff training. We are using the results of the buildingwide formal walkabout and an external evaluation as the basis for improvements being negotiated with the State Office of General Services and the Division of Budget.

Questions We Must Ask

You recall that the ALA publication *Planning and Role Setting for Public Libraries* uses the phrase "looking around" to describe the process of collecting information about the library and its community.[3] The questions it poses are a starting point for general community study for a public library or a school or academic library. They are also the starting point for planning, and with appropriate adaptation, can be used to look closely at any sector of the community, including people with disabilities.

We can translate those questions to: What is this community? Who comprises it? Where do they live? What are their needs? What problems do they have and what barriers do they encounter in using the library? Those questions lead to a closer look at the library and its capacity for serving.

How are we communicating with our community? What can we do to reduce barriers to make services more accessible? In examining service for people with disabilities, we need to investigate particularly:

- opportunity for electronic access from home or workstation and for delivery of printed audio and video materials;
- availability of adaptive devices to compensate for failed vision, hearing, coordination, etc.;
- getting into the library—parking, walks, ramps, entrances, and doors;
- using the library—tables, service counters, aisles, collections, equipment, signs, meeting spaces, restrooms, stairs, elevators, lighting, and floors;
- behind the scenes—switches, safety devices, water fountains, telephones, lockers, and coat racks.[4]

Additional Sources of Information and Help

The State Library of Florida publication, *Surveying Public Libraries for the ADA*, is certainly a document that we need to use (see appendix A). In addition to that and these other things, I urge you to check with your customers—the people with disabilities—and with the local agencies, organizations, and key state agencies. Even after you acquire that two-inch-thick bible, *The Americans with Disabilities Handbook*,[5] ask locally about the materials on the ADA. Asking helps you make contacts with people who care and who are ready to serve the community.

In each state, there is an agency, usually in the department of education, responsible for vocational rehabilitation, and that agency is ready to help with information, training, advice, and context. There is likely another state agency that functions as an advocate for people with disabilities.

Today's Curb Cuts

At last year's White House conference, Deborah Kaplan, associate director of public education at the World Institute on Disability, described how improvements made for people with disabilities benefit the general public.[6] She pointed out that sidewalk curb cuts that were once so controversial and seen as so expensive are now used as often by parents with baby strollers, kids on skateboards, delivery people moving off their loads and others. Kaplan also talked about our need for what she called "electronic curb cuts," as we explore computer-based information technology.

She described how technology has changed the lives of people who are blind. As I listened to her, I thought of the 1978 White House conference. The breakthrough at that point was the Kurzweil reading machine and its electronic scanning and synthesized speech. Today it's voice synthesizing based on ASCII text and graphics technology. Through the Internet, people with a computer and modem at home will be downloading databases from libraries throughout that Internet and using their voice synthesizers to read that information.

Kaplan's point is that we need to look at

technology for our total community and see people with disabilities as an important part of that total community. We can use technology to serve people with disabilities better than libraries ever have served any users before.

An online catalog available to a person with a home computer and modem, as is now available in the Mohawk Valley library system, is an effective way of rendering geographic and physical barriers irrelevant. Telecommunications and the Internet enable the user to be at the center of the information service network. The electronic doorway library enables people to get service from their homes, locate widely dispersed information, and communicate with individuals at affinity groups.[7]

One of this year's most important developments in the technology-based service to people with disabilities is the formation of a committee of network directors, headed by Glyn Evans, vice-chancellor of the State University of New York, who also is the director of the SUNY/OCLC network in New York State. He is working with a committee of directors to prepare a guide for electronic services particularly geared toward meeting information needs of people with disabilities. Equal Access to Software for Instruction (EASI) is publishing information of interest to academics who have in their community some four and a half million students with disabilities.

First Results

I expect that your plan will start with something simple and noticeable. It might be something as practical as moving reference books to the edge of tables and off tall stands, or widening the aisles between tables to at least thirty-six inches. Laura Flynn, the librarian at the Fort Plain Public Library, which serves about twenty-five hundred people in the Mohawk Valley library system, expanded the library building in 1984. That library is a Greek revival house built in the 1820s. They added space to it, and, in addition to the new space, she made sure the library was accessible, included spring-operated automatic doors.

But about four years later, as a result of a walkabout with the help of customers with disabilities, she found some surprising barriers. She saw that it would help people in wheelchairs if she moved a bookcase and a copying machine. She could also help them if she lowered the towel dispenser and wrapped the hot water pipes in the lavatory. None of these changes cost money, she points out, but they are important to library users.

You will come up with practical immediate things to do to make a start. Let everyone know you are serious about access and involve them in as many ways as you can. Many community groups that are not directly concerned with disabilities may have a more general, but important, role to help in making services accessible. Your staff, users, and trustees may be aware of citizen projects undertaken by the Girl Scouts, Boy Scouts, 4-H, Lions, and other groups— people of all ages. None of us has the money to do all the jobs that they volunteer for and are willing to do. The more help we can marshal, the better.

The first steps will include a function almost every library does well: providing information. People from all walks of life need information about disabilities, nutrition, health care, jobs. Of course, they need not necessarily come to the library for information.

Telephone reference services is overlooked by many people in our community. Most libraries can provide specialized reference services and database services by requesting them from the library system, the state library, or other organizations. At the least, staff in any library can identify sources in other libraries.

First steps may also include the staff informing itself on such resources as talking books, new systems for informing parents about developmental disabilities, the databases, inexpensive adaptive equipment and resources available in the community.

In the course of planning, particularly as you use the *Americans with Disabilities Act Handbook*, you will develop administrative questions relating to resource management, standards, budgeting, public information, complaints policies, and staff.

A Recipe for Success

Deep in our hearts, many of us seek the recipe for success, particularly when there is so much work to be done.

At the outset, I used some figures to suggest possibilities for enlarging our service and serving a greater number of people in our community. What I hope these figures suggest is the potential for serving people who have, in many instances, been bypassed by library services. We know there are many people we want to draw into the libraries and many whom we want to serve without their needing to come to the library.

Ultimately, people make their own decisions on whether or not they want to use our libraries. The only two types of libraries to which some people are compelled to come are prison libraries and some school libraries. We want to make sure that they make their choice of using or not using a library with full information on what the library can do for them and that they have the assurance that the library services are available to them.

As I prepared for this conference, I was thinking about the reasons that people with disabilities have not been as well served as we now see necessary. At that point, I wrote that people with disabilities have not been as well served because they were, in a sense, not sufficiently visible, assertive, and political. In the metaphor of Virginia Woolf, "they were there, but they were Shakespeare's sister"—the Elizabethan women.[8] I stick that in a room of one's own. She was describing the disability of women in general, specifically their invisibility.

Michael Gunde, the assistant library director and the Florida director of Library Services for the Blind, said as much in a provocative article with the disarming title, "What Every Librarian Should Know about the Americans with Disabilities Act." He takes the library profession to task for preaching outreach but more often practicing exclusion that has resulted in discrimination against individuals with disabilities. He warns that we may pay dearly for litigation, perceptual problems that result from reluctant responses to client needs, and legal mandates. He concludes that:

> Libraries, of course, should have always provided equitable services to people with disabilities, if for no other reasons than that our own professional ethics require it, most library mission statements imply it, and, to some extent, the fiscal health of our institutions depends upon it.[9]

The other side of Gunde's point is that service to people with disabilities draws support. Politically skilled advocates need help with bond issues to levy public support for service to the total community. Service to particular segments of the community also often leverages support from foundations or corporate sources.

The ADA is a powerful stimulus for us to look again at our community and to reach out to people who can help us serve others with information and library services needs. If there is a recipe for success, it is that we serve a wider community; that we provide that service in a client centered, quality management approach; and that we recognize the clear connections to our mission and the vitality of our community.

David Esquith mentioned a really important part of this session dialogue and questions. I want to tell you about this little folder called "Now That We've Met, What Do I Say?" It was developed by Josh Cohen of the Mid-Hudson Library System, who brought a few copies to this conference. If you haven't seen it, don't hesitate to contact him in Poughkeepsie, New York.

References and Notes

1. Equal Access to Software for Instruction, *EASI Computer Access Facts* (project of EDUCOM Educational Uses of Information Technology Program). EDUCOM, 1112 16th St., NW, Suite 600, Washington, DC 20036.
2. Sara Dallas, "Independent Living Centers and the Public Library," *The Bookmark* 46, no.4 (Summer 1988): 261–64.
3. Charles R. McClure and others, *Planning and Role Setting for Public Libraries: A Manual of Options and Procedures* (Chicago: ALA, 1987).
4. Three of these points are taken from the following publication: Marianne Kotch Cassell and the Vermont Board of Libraries Access Task Force, *Planning for Accessibility* (Montpelier, Vt.: Vermont Department of Libraries, 1991), 69.
5. U.S. Equal Opportunity Commission and the U.S. Department of Justice, *American with Disabilities Handbook* (Washington, D.C.: Govt. Print. Off., 1991).
6. Deborah Kaplan, remarks to the White House Conference on Library and Information Science, Washington, D.C., July 10, 1991.
7. New York State Library-NYSERNet Joint Planning Team, *Libraries, Librarians, and Networked Services: A Vision Statement for the Electronic Doorway Library* (Albany, N.Y.: New York State Library, 1992), 1.
8. Virginia Woolf, *A Room of One's Own* (New York: Harcourt, 1929), 44–51.
9. Michael Gunde, "What Every Librarian Should Know about the Americans with Disabilities Act," *American Libraries* 22 (Sept. 1991): 806–809.

Social Implications for Disabled and Nondisabled People

Judith Heumann

I would like to say that libraries have always been a very important part of my life. I guess at least of my fantasy life. One of my jobs at the World Institute, which is a research and policy and educational institution, is to direct the research and training center. The other day when I was talking to staff about the presentation I was going to be giving, we started talking about the role of libraries. It became evident to me and a number of other staff who had more significant disabilities that people of my age have really had limited ability to use libraries the way nondisabled individuals do.

That's been a major loss for myself and other people. I'm hoping that meetings like this would incorporate disabled people into this area. I know that librarians and others are doing some very good work. I would like to underscore that as the Americans with Disabilities Act becomes a reality, along with many other pieces of legislation that we have been working on, libraries are going to play a more and more integrated role in ensuring that disabled individuals can become integrated members of society.

It's critically important you recognize that your jobs are more important than those in many other fields out in the world; knowledge is critical to all of us. You obviously understand that as nondisabled individuals. Loss of access to knowledge is something that is going to prevent us greatly from really being able to become part of our community. Legislation like the Americans with Disabilities Act has begun to allow us to look at this area.

Many of you, like myself, are working to transform our communities into places where all people, regardless of age, race and ethnicity, sexual orientation, or disability, can participate in all facets of society, free from discrimination, with equal opportunity for all.

When I was asked to address you on the Americans with Disabilities Act and other victories, I knew I would not be able to come here and paint you a picture of instant equality for all disabled people. When I examine the past and look critically at the present, I realize that the challenge we face is much deeper than simply legislating discrimination away.

We must all look at our own prejudice, our own roles in the systemic oppression that disabled people face. Only by rooting out our own biases will the future of true equality be possible.

The past twenty years have seen major advances in legislation for disabled people. I and thousands of other disabled people and friends all across the country have fought hard and won victories with passage of the Americans with Disabilities Act, the educational legislation, Section 504 of the Rehabilitation Act, legislation perceived by independent living centers, and in-home, support-service funding. These extremely important pieces of legislation are producing important changes. Today, if I were five years old and my mother took me to my local school, the staff would not be allowed to dismiss me as a fire hazard, send me home with two hours of teacher visits a week, and call

---

Judith Heumann is Vice-President of the World Institute on Disability.

that education. They would have curb cuts in streets throughout the country. Buses are becoming accessible, and buildings are being constructed with ramps, elevators, wide doorways, and accessible bathrooms. Closed captioning for television is also becoming a reality. These meaningful structural changes are taking care of a very visible and essential piece of our fight for equal access.

In 1990, the Census Bureau released statistics on the number of disabled people who are employed. Fewer disabled people are working now than in the early 1980s. The unemployment rate for disabled people is 70 percent— not 17 percent, but 70 percent.

Forty percent of disabled children are dropping out before graduating from high school, and indications are that the number of disabled students attending colleges and universities is also decreasing. I was alarmed by these figures, as I assume you are.

With such a number of landmark pieces of legislation, why are we not seeing dramatic changes in the quality of disabled people's lives? I believe we are not seeing these dramatic changes yet because society as a whole has not made the commitment necessary to truly provide equal opportunities. This lack of commitment, I believe, stems from an unwillingness to acknowledge that society does, in fact, perceive disabled individuals as inferior.

Recently, a friend of mine who is an employer was telling me some disturbing true stories I would like to share with you. Both took place in California.

One concerned a court reporter with a back injury who required a custom-designed chair from his employer. Although his supervisor, a judge, agreed to the request, the legal department decided that this was a personal item and not the employer's responsibility to purchase, as they didn't want to set a precedent. The State Attorney General's office had to get involved before the court administrator would agree to spend $350 on the chair. Thousands of dollars were spent fighting an individual's attempt to continue working. Thousands of dollars were spent fighting the prejudice and discrimination of one court administrator.

How many other similar stories to this one end in frustration for disabled people who are unused and unwilling to deal with this type of bureaucracy and discrimination? How many would be able to find an attorney to assist them in handling this relatively simple case? How many people should need to even consider getting an attorney to handle something that should have just been done without any second thought?

The second case concerns a young girl with mild mental retardation who had been successfully integrated into a kindergarten in a public school. Her parents wanted her to attend an arts public school, continuing in an integrated setting for which she would need a part-time aide. The school district insisted she be placed in a special education class.

I would like to just stop for a second and say I don't like the word *special*. I really wish it was a word that could be removed because, I think, when you think about special, you think about something that is different. When we think about special, all too frequently we don't think about it in a positive way. We think about it as a burden and something we don't want to have to deal with in economically strapped times. So, I feel if the word *special* were removed, it would allow us to begin to think about disabled individuals as being a part of whatever work we are doing.

Getting back to the story of this young girl: The school district insisted that she be placed in a special education class. After twelve days of fair hearing, with three corporate attorneys, the school district lost. The school district appealed; the school district lost. Did you see the "LA Law" story? It was the same scenario. The school district is once again appealing.

Such actions negatively affect disabled children and their nondisabled peers. The school district's lack of flexibility is unfortunately still too typical an approach to dealing with the integration of disabled people.

How many of you, when hearing this case, think that perhaps the school district is correct? After all, they have had more experience dealing with these type of special children than her parents did. Wouldn't she benefit from special teachers, special experts in helping Karen with her special needs? The reality is that separate but equal cannot be tolerated in any area, particularly in education, our libraries, and our community as a whole.

The failure to integrate disabled and nondisabled people at an early age will continue to result in nondisabled adults who fear difference and lack understanding, and disabled adults who fear integration and lack self-respect.

I'm getting married this summer and looking for a place to get married. We are having a small wedding of about 250 people. I have many friends who are also in wheelchairs. So, I'm looking for a place that can accommodate fifty to eighty people in wheelchairs. On the East Coast it's not such a difficult thing to do, but in our area in California it is.

I found a beautiful place that a number of people recommended to me; someone told me the place was accessible. We went out there and it was really gorgeous; it was exactly the place where I wanted to be married. They told me, "no difficulty"; they could handle about 400 to 500 people standing, and 250 people, 60 to 70 people in wheelchairs, was no problem at all.

As I went through the facility, which was a house, I noticed two little lips that were no more than two and a half inches, and a step of about four inches. I said, "We will need to take care of these two lips and this step." The manager replied, "Oh, I really don't know if we can do that. I think that might cost much too much money."

The reality was it wasn't going to cost too much money at all. She didn't want to make the changes. This was a very interesting experience because I know what the law requires. I know it's not an undue hardship and I know she has been required to do this in California, separately from the federal law.

I wanted that place, and I also knew that there was another group that wanted it the same day I did. I tried to figure out how to negotiate this because she could easily have turned around and told me, "We already gave it away. They came forward before you did." I tried, in a very polite, politically appropriate way, to discuss this with her. So I said, "Oh, well, you know I don't think it's going to be a big deal." I hemmed and hawed, and I looked at another place, which was just not as nice as the first place. I looked at I can't tell you how many other places.

I had someone call her and say we wanted to take the place. She responded that the fire marshal said we couldn't have 250 people with 60 people in wheelchairs. I had a friend call a couple of days later to say she was looking to book a place for October for 250 to 300 people. "No problem," the manager said. "Standing or sitting?" Anything. "No problem. We can handle more than that." That's all I needed to hear.

We are not using the place, but I am speaking to an attorney, and I'm telling you this because it's this type of situation that did not need to occur. The changes that this woman needs to make to her place are nonsignificant, but she has a very strong mindset about what she is willing to do. It's very much like the example of the $350 chair.

I think these are the kinds of examples that you or your peers come across, maybe sometimes you participate in them, maybe sometimes you really don't like hearing about them, but they are the kinds of stories that we are plagued with every day of our lives.

Causes of discrimination against disabled people have some unique twists. Nondisabled people fear disability. They do not want to face the possibility or probability that at some point they, too, may become disabled.

One might hate women or African-Americans or Asians or Latinos or Jews or Catholics or gay people, but there is no fear of waking up some morning being one of them. I have had disabled friends tell me some of the thoughts they had about disability when they were not disabled. Thoughts such as, I would rather be dead than be in a wheelchair, or what a shame that such a beautiful person is disabled. I don't know how I could live my life like that. What a burden that person must be upon family and friends. Imagine how you would feel if someone walked up to you and said, as they did to a friend of mine, "What's a pretty girl like you doing in a wheelchair?" The obvious retort is, "What's a good-looking boy like you doing walking?"

A coworker who used a wheelchair in high school was approached by a nondisabled student who said, "If I'm ever like you, I hope they shoot me."

This pernicious fear that grips many nondisabled people makes those of us with disabilities angry, ashamed, humiliated, unwanted, and, in extreme cases, fearful for our very lives.

One way of considering some of these issues is to ask yourself, What disability am I most afraid of? Then try to see yourself with that disability. What happens to you? Do you feel like you are losing control, see your life dramatically changing before your eyes, feel like your life is becoming worthless? Why? Why do you worry about it? You worry about how your friends are going to react to you, about how you are going to react to yourself? What is your fear? How do you respond to it? Are you aware of community organizations and government programs that are available to help you? Are you a part of resolving these problems, so that if you would become disabled, disability is not a fear to you because you have been involved in helping to make changes that allow you to be a person who has a disability and live like anybody else?

I have presented many examples of barriers that disabled people face in order to help you understand the systemic discrimination that we still are facing on a day-to-day basis. Like other minority groups, we finally have recognized that we have to begin to work together as disabled people. We are persevering. We are working together to create organizations like Independent Living Centers, World Institute on Disability, the Disability Rights Education Defense Fund, and many others. These organizations, which are run by disabled people, are helping us gain the self-esteem that so many of us have never had or have lost along the way. We have been working with disabled people and their families to encourage them to fight for what they believe is right and just: equality and integration in our community.

In 1975, a report of the United Nations expert group meeting on design stated:

> Despite everything we can do, or hope to do, to assist each physically and mentally disabled person reach his or her maximum potential in life, our efforts will not succeed until we have found the way to remove the obstacles directed by human society: the physical barriers we have created in public buildings, housing, transportation, houses of worship, of social life and other community facilities; social barriers we evolved and accepted against those who vary more than a certain degree from what [we had been conditioned to regard as normal].

More people are forced into limited lives and made to suffer by these man-made obstacles than by any specific physical or mental disability. Together we must continue to work for a better world, free of these obstacles.

I hope that this presentation has convinced you that you can play a meaningful role in helping to eliminate discrimination against disabled people. I would encourage you to begin to look at what you as individuals do consciously or unconsciously to perpetuate this prejudice and discrimination against disabled people.

For example, does your library actively recruit disabled people to work? Are you advancing disabled individuals in employment? Are you encouraging disabled individuals to go into the field of library science at the university level? Are your facilities wheelchair accessible? If there is a need for money, are you encouraging disabled people to work with you in your community to raise the money that's necessary to make your facility accessible? Do you consider prejudice against disabled people to be equivalent in importance to other forms of discrimination? Do you resent having to make changes in your programs in a tight fiscal time?

I hope, and I personally look forward to being able, to work with you and others around the country in making the dream of ADA become a reality. I encourage you to get a little magazine called the *Disability Rag.* I read a great piece in there by John Hockenberry, a reporter for public radio who uses a wheelchair. Maybe some of you saw the editorial that appeared in the *New York Times* when he was thrown out of a theater. He has a profound piece in the *Disability Rag* that talks about how he and other people are facing discrimination. I think about how we as a people are working to overcome those forms of discrimination.

We welcome very much the opportunity to work with you. Librarians, in my mind, hold the keys to knowledge and you really must help us open those doors.

Exemplary Library Programs and Services for Those with Disabilities

Phyllis Dalton

We librarians have always believed in library service for all, including people with disabilities, and now we have it legislated in the Americans with Disabilities Act (ADA). What I'm going to talk about today is library programs and services and the Americans with Disabilities Act.

A well-known poem by Robert Frost, *Stopping by Woods on a Snowy Evening*, concludes:

The woods are lovely, dark and deep,
But I have promises to keep,
And miles to go before I sleep,
And miles to go before I sleep.

Those of us who have been working with library services for people with disabilities have made many promises, and we hope to keep them all. It is true, however, that there are miles and miles to go before we achieve our objectives.

I shall briefly review some of our libraries' best work in that field—work that is to be continued, to be emulated, or to be challenged by the exemplary programs and services that others are providing or will provide. All of the material that I'm using has been gathered firsthand within the last six months from the person managing the program in some way. Therefore, it is as current as possible given distance, time, and other limiting factors. Appendix B provides a list of twenty-seven library programs and the person you can contact, because I will give you only a little bit about each program today.

To begin developing programs and services in keeping with the ADA, we have to start at the beginning, the very beginning, and take the very first step. I have chosen the Scottsdale Public Library in Arizona, where I live, as the best example of how to start implementing the ADA.

At the Arizona Library Association conference in late 1991, Bill Scott, the founder of Abilities Unlimited, spoke on ADA and libraries. Soon after that, Linda Saferite, the public library director of the Scottsdale system, asked me to speak to the Scottsdale Public Library administrators. We had a very good free-flowing session.

Linda appointed Connie Mulholland, library systems manager, to be the focal person for the ADA. A most effective citizen committee was appointed to work with Connie. Two of the five members use wheelchairs, as does the consultant to the committee. I'm one of the five, and I have many of what are known as deficits as the result of brain surgeries. Each of the five persons, as well as the resources person, is well versed in the ADA and is committed to the best in library service for all people in Scottsdale.

The committee reviewed carefully the library plans for new construction, evaluated the present buildings and services, met with the city officials who were concerned specifically with the ADA, and recommended implementations, continuing to do so as the work progresses. There is no waiting for the committee to issue a report. The changes are now in place or the planning is being done for them.

Phyllis Dalton is a library consultant.

What are libraries doing that will enable them to meet the needs of Americans with disabilities? I shall give you quick vignettes of the work being done so you can follow up as you wish.

A two-tiered approach to providing comprehensive library service to people with disabilities is being used by the Montgomery County Public Library in Maryland. Agnes Griffin is the director. In that library system, accommodation is a part of regular library service, allowing people to use the resources of every branch and all special collections.

If a special format or service is beyond the scope of the library where the initial contact is made, the Special Needs library staff assists the patron. I agree with Judy, there should be a better word than *special*, but I have never found it. Even this organization uses the word *specialized* in its name.

Funding for all special services is included as a nondesignated part of the department's operational budget. All services to people with disabilities are mainstreamed whenever possible. Staff members attend workshops on accommodation, which include an open discussion about access with those who speak from personal experience. Some special assistive devices available are magnifiers and TDD (telecommunication device for the deaf, or as it's also known now, text telephone [TT]). As was shown, not everyone is deaf who uses the TDD or TT, closed-circuit television readers, or meeting rooms with assistive listening devices.

The library is planning ahead to make the public access catalog accessible to people who do not use print. A special brochure, *A Handbook for Volunteers*, is an excellent publication of the Montgomery County Public Library.

The second library, and one with which I have had personal experience, that has a special needs center providing comprehensive services to people with disabilities is the Phoenix Public Library in Arizona. This library has many services that make mainstreaming possible.

One area of service that has proved most useful is the computer workplace and the access to print that technology provides. They have recently interfaced the public online catalog with a computer that has speech capabilities and are able, as a result, to provide users who are blind and visually impaired with access to the library collection. Their new Kurzweil Personal Reader is easy to use but takes some training. Users are designing training sessions for those who have not used a Kurzweil. The same computer with speech has a braille translation program as well as being interfaced with a braille embosser and a braille display on the screen so that users who prefer braille may work in that format.

Another use of technology is the public TDD and the lending of closed caption decoders. Anyone who is hearing impaired and wishes to make a long distance telephone call can just plug the TDD into a pay phone.

The term *access center* describes the center even better than *special needs*. The library system tries to meet the needs of people with disabilities as their point of contact with the library. This is possible because it's accessible, on the first floor. When this is not possible, or special technology is needed, the center provides the access. The library also has special staff training on the ADA.

Another service is the Toybrary, a free toy lending service to parents of children with disabilities or to the professionals who work with children. The emphasis is that toys are not just for play. Children gather information about their world through toys. I can tell you from talking to some of the toy dolls that they are very user friendly.

Because disabilities and illnesses sometimes prevent people from coming to the library, the Berkeley Public Library in California provides the service called "If You Can't Come to Us, We'll Come to You." This delivery system, which makes 160 visits per month, is about twenty years old. Although it certainly predates ADA, it is done in the spirit of ADA. This program has been funded from the library budget since 1980. A part of this important program is staff training to increase sensitivity, understanding, and communication skills, as well as to provide a knowledge of attitudinal and architectural barriers.

The staff is trained and knows about accommodations to provide equal access to people who are disabled. A part of the training is provided by the Berkeley residents who understand disabilities through their own experiences. Experience with this program by both the library and the user is that it is highly successful.

A second such service is provided by the Los Angeles Public Library in a program known simply as "Service to Shut-ins." It is financed by the library budget. It is most significant that this program is operated in all of the sixty-two branches as well as in the Central Library. Five hundred volunteers circulate approximately twelve thousand items each month to over one thousand individuals. The program is provided to people who, because of disability or illness, cannot come to the library. The library provides an outstanding information folder titled "Service to Shut-ins."

To provide service to the people who are developmentally disabled, the Pioneer Library System in Newark, a cooperative public library system serving four counties, has set up "Bridges to the Community." It serves a rural community with a population of just under three hundred thousand. A valuable part of this service is making available a collection of theme kits that contain books, video cassettes, manipulates, games, and ideas for the use of the kit.

A most important part of the work with people who are developmentally disabled is finding just the right contact person within the area. The system has found that making one correct contact brings in many more. Some of these contact persons have been recreational therapists, social workers, staff development personnel, and psychologists. A workshop to sensitize library personnel to informational and recreational needs of people with disabilities is an important part of the service.

This program is supported by the Library Services and Construction Act, (LSCA) funds. The purposes are, one: it serves to provide more information on developmental disabilities, and two: it enables work to be carried out successfully with individuals who are developmentally disabled.

Because a diploma is so important in securing employment, the Library for the Blind and Physically Handicapped of The Free Library of Philadelphia has a GED program. It has the important mission of enabling disabled adults who are seeking to complete their high school education to do so by earning a General Equivalency Diploma. During the past fiscal year, the program has had a 72 percent increase in enrollment and eleven adults have received their diplomas.

A special "I CAN! Center" at the San Diego Public Library is still in its infancy but is expanding its services as rapidly as possible. It is in the process of purchasing several telecaption decoders that will be made available for public use in the library and its branches. A Kurzweil machine will be acquired also.

Presently, the clientele is small. It is growing as people learn about the availability of this service. Highlights of the present program are a six-thousand–volume large-print collection, a talking book program, and consultation services. A color video magnifier CCTV, which magnifies up to sixty times, amplified public telephones, and telecommunication devices for the deaf (TDD) are all available for people to use. Approximately four hundred closed-captioned videocassette titles that may be borrowed are in the collection. Sign language interpreters are available.

The center is also a networking source for agencies, advocates, schools, employers, and people with disabilities. This networking is done through newsletters, catalogs, meetings, referrals, and a compilation of resource directories. Although the emphasis is on visual and hearing impairments, people with other disabilities are encouraged to come and are accommodated.

The New York Public Library offers the Office of Special Services with a number of programs and services in both the main library and in the branches for people who are disabled. "Project Access," which is housed in the Mid-Manhattan Library, offers, in addition to the services mentioned, a wheelchair available for public use, adjustable study tables, book holders, and manual page turners, as well as recorded career information and library orientation materials in braille and on cassette. They also have a collection of materials including directories of organizations and services to people who are disabled and pamphlets covering such topics as advocacy, accessibility, independent living, and travel.

There are newsletters describing the new technologies and legislative developments, plus sources for materials in special formats. An excellent service is a pamphlet addressed to staff on how to serve people with disabilities called "Making Contact." Disabilities are covered in general, with special information on visual impairment, deafness and hearing impairment, mobility impairment, and developmental impairment, as well as services and equipment. There is a notation to the staff to forget phrases such as *afflicted with, victim of,* and *confined to.* Two especially noteworthy items are the statement to the staff that "Libraries serve people, not percentages" and that "Knowing How to Serve People with Disabilities" is noted among the skills listed that make a good staff member.

The Seattle Public Library has a similar program. It administers the "Library Equal Access Program" with the acronym LEAP. This is a permanent program funded from the library budget and emphasizes services to people who are visually impaired, hearing impaired, or deaf. The Kurzweil machine, the speech synthesizer computer, and other adaptive aids are part of the program. The program provides a TDD and closed-caption decoders that are available for borrowing.

In other outreach efforts of LEAP, many individuals with disabilities are being contacted and served. The LEAP program has clearly indicated that information access, of which the ADA certainly speaks, has furthered the independence of individuals through adaptive equipment and has improved their access to many resources. LEAP first started with an LSCA grant.

The San Francisco Public Library has a program, launched in 1978 with an LSCA grant, which provides "Services to the Deaf and Hearing Impaired." Although it is an early program in this field, it is constantly forward looking. The effort made in establishing a TDD story line resulted in making children who are deaf able to access the stories just like their hearing peers can.

The collection of materials there is outstanding. They range from children's storybooks to weighty tomes on linguistics. Some of the excellent tapes in the collection have been produced by the San Francisco Public Library. Two are the award-winning *Language Landscapes* and the four-tape series titled *American Culture: The Deaf Perspective*.

One college library that is fortunate to be on a barrier-free campus is the Ramapo College of New Jersey at Mahwah. Also barrier free is the library, which has taken into consideration from the very beginning the needs of persons with disabilities. Some of the features of the building are book stacks with wide passageways, doors that open automatically, and restrooms with the proper equipment. The college library staff and the special services for the college work together to provide equal access to people with disabilities to library programs and services.

A second such library is the Appalachian State University in Boone, North Carolina, where the university is engaged in an ongoing renovation to remove barriers between the campus buildings and within the buildings.

The program is funded with university funds. The library offers the services of the Kurzweil reading machine, Information through Speech (ITS), the talking computer, the braille calculator, and the talking calculator. Braille material is available also, including the *Websters New World Dictionary of the American Language* in seventy-one volumes, and this same publication in large print in twenty-four volumes. The library also has amassed a collection of publications dealing with legal, social, educational, and operational issues confronting people with disabilities.

I'll mention three state libraries. The Vermont State Library has published *Planning for Accessibility*, which is designed to get librarians and trustees started to address physical access to the library by people with disabilities. It has just been issued and is a project of the Vermont Board of Libraries Task Force. It includes excerpts from the Americans with Disabilities Act of interest to public libraries and also other laws and regulations relating to people who are disabled. Covered are such topics as low-cost changes such as the requirements for parking, walks, ramps, and other physical barriers to disabilities.

There is a pilot project for outpatients who are mentally ill in process at the Pennsylvania State Library, funded by the Library Services and Construction Act. The needs of the people have been identified as choice of vocation, how to survive in an open society, literacy, and socializing skills. The library will have four computerized "wellness stations," which will concentrate on these needs. In November 1992, the outpatient library staff will report their findings to the Pennsylvania Library Association.

A third state library included is the Utah State Library, which maintains a corps of volunteer readers for the production of textbooks as a special service to students. The library has also established a volunteer recording program in each of the four major universities and in the state prison. The library will tape braille or large-print students textbooks in any programs in the state.

Two libraries with radio stations as a prominent part of their programs are in Tennessee—the Memphis/Shelby County Public Library and Information Center and the Nashville and Davidson County Library. In Memphis, the library, along with radio station WYPL, has made information available by using special workstations. The FM channel reaches over a million listeners within a fifty-mile radius. Users can utilize technology to access information with six workstations. They are the Kurzweil, the Visualtek Magnification, the Large Print/Physically Disabled, the braille computer, the Magnification, and the Media Training Center.

In Nashville, radio station WPLN participated with the public library's reading program.

WPLN also has a Talking Library, which is a a radio reading service broadcast twenty-four hours a day the year round.

In 8,760 hours of programming, magazines; local, regional, and national newspapers; and 113 books were read. An experimental program of audio-described movies was broadcast. This included two films: *Robin Hood* and *Casablanca*. A special reading of the books *Dances with Wolves* and *Awakenings*, on which the movies were based, was aired.

Here are snapshots of several other library programs. The Worcester County Library in Maryland will comply with the ADA by continuing its usual policy of staff not staying behind the desk but rather accompanying the individuals to the stacks. This method of staff operation allows equal access. The basic library function involves active communication with all patrons. Staff will be aware of the patron needs and respond in an appropriate manner.

"Helping Hand: Deaf Awareness," a program at the Onandaga Library, New York, involves employing a qualified interpreter to work at the central library. The use of the interpreter attracts more people who are deaf and hearing impaired to use library services. It makes the services available to twelve hundred deaf and hearing-impaired students.

A highly successful use of technology in the Robinson Township Public Library District, Illinois, resulted in the staff recommending strongly that public libraries of all sizes consider offering talking computer access to their patrons who are reading impaired. Success with people who are visually impaired or with dyslexia prompted them to make this recommendation.

In Charlottesville, Virginia, the Jefferson/Madison Regional Library has a program of group visits for adults who are mentally retarded. The day care center is within blocks of the library. They use the entire library and select the materials at the level most appropriate to their needs. Each person has his or her own library card.

The North Suburban Library System in Wheeling, Illinois, has a unique and very successful program called the "Skokie Accessible Library Service Project" (SALS).

A great program in the Hennepin County Library in Minnesota is a children's program. The programs in this series are interpreted for children who are deaf or otherwise hearing impaired. Voice interpreters are also available, as well as sign language interpreters. In putting the new project together, the library contacted well over nineteen organizations to secure people who are deaf or hearing impaired, not only to find the children who could benefit from the program, but to help publicize the service as well. Two excellent video programs are provided by the library for staff training. These are "Deaf Awareness" and "Sensitivity to the Disabled Patron."

The Pike's Peak Library District in Colorado inaugurated the "Challenged Child Reading Center." This provides a place where ignorance about children who are disabled can be dispelled as well as a place where parents of the children can meet for enjoyment and shared experience and knowledge. The center houses a broad and exciting range of books for professionals, adults, and children. Some of the subjects in the computer base are mental health/restoration, developmental disabilities, dystrophy, speech/language therapy, learning disabilities, and prematurity.

The library issued a bibliography titled *You Can't Judge a Book by Its Cover*, which is all about challenged children. Books in the library collection feature information on cerebral palsy, Down's syndrome, spina bifida, autism, learning disabilities, and disabilities in general.

The Atlanta-Fulton Public Library Learning Center is financed through the library budget. This center is designed in part to provide library service to people who are visually or hearing impaired or both. Provided are a Kurzweil reading machine; a Visualtek, an electronic print enlarger; large-print books, magazines, and newspapers; and cassettes and magnifiers. For people with hearing problems, a TDD is available, along with instructional sign language, videotapes on sign language, and a referral service. A special feature of the project is a program to improve an individual's test taking ability in preparation for employment.

The Cleveland Public Library for the Blind and Physically Handicapped Library developed a CD-ROM reference service for their patrons. The CD-ROM database offers new information in large type and braille for those whose vision difficulties makes them unable to use conventional printed sources. This system combines a PC laser drive and the CD-ROM. For those who can't come to the library, a toll-free number can be called to request large-type or braille printouts from such reference materials as *McGraw-Hill Science and Technology Encyclopedia*, *Grolier's Electronic Encyclopedia*, *Word Cruncher*, both the King James version and the New International version of the Bible, the *Ri-*

verside Shakespeare, and the *Physician's Desk Reference.*

A CD-ROM player coupled with braille translating software and a laser printer can turn articles from reference works such as those mentioned above into braille and large print in a matter of minutes. A voice card inserted in the PC allows visually impaired people to listen to the articles.

Just as I was finishing my work on all of this, in *Silent News,* in the section "Around the USA," under Illinois, I read the following:

> The Skokie Public Library has adopted a resolution of compliance with the Americans with Disabilities Act as a means of renewing its commitment to serving disabled members of the public.
>
> "We have been very progressive thus far in our effort to serve disabled people," says Director Carolyn Anthony. Leslie Williams will coordinate compliance with the ADA.

It was the only entry under Illinois. I was very proud of libraries.

Just as I was coming here, I received this wonderful information about the Library Services and Construction Act and the Americans with Disabilities Act, which I am sure go hand in hand. This was in Illinois with Joe Natale, Title II LSCA coordinator at the Illinois State Library. His telephone number is (217) 782-7749.

The libraries in this project are as follows: The Pekin Public Library, Pekin, Illinois, was granted $19,100 for a project remodeling restrooms located in the main lobby area to comply with ADA. The work will bring the entire library into compliance.

The Summit Public Library District, Summit, Illinois, has a project costing $26,774. With this project the library will correct structural deficiencies by remodeling restrooms, installing miscellaneous hardware, doors, and water fountains.

The Galena Public Library, Galena, Illinois, has a project for the sum of $265,733. The library there is a Carnegie Public Library. I think it's very interesting that we can successfully go from Carnegie to ADA. In making a Carnegie library accessible all the formidable steps are no longer a barrier. It will be brought into compliance with ADA and the Illinois Accessibility Code with construction of an elevator, remodeling restrooms, and moving shelves to allow forty-two-inch aisles.

Shorewood-Troy Public Library District, Shorewood, Illinois, has a project fund of $160,824 to provide access to the lower level of the library by the installation of an elevator and accessible restrooms. Both levels will have special equipment, furniture, and signage for people with disabilities.

Then there is a new project with a project expenditure of $1,347,360 for the University Park Public Library District in University Park, Illinois, for new a facility of ten thousand square feet to be constructed in compliance with ADA. The new library will allow for the expansion of the library collection and there will be a meeting room.

All of these projects conform to the Illinois State Library's long-range plan as recommended by the Illinois State Library Advisory Committee and its subcommittee for library construction.

A program was received very recently from the Brooklyn Public Library. The name of the project is "The Child's Place for Children with Special Needs."

In 1978, the library designated certain branches as centers for work with preschool children. These centers were known as "The Child's Place." In 1988 this service was extended to children with special needs and was located at a "Child's Place" in the Flatland Branch. The library is completely accessible, with special furniture, adapted toys, and books that are appropriate for the children who use them.

There is also a selection of books for parents and caregivers. The target group is aged from birth to nine years, and the program is attended by children with autism, speech and language disorders, cerebral palsy, developmental disabilities, learning disabilities, and multiple disabilities. The programs include class visits, story time, and toys for tots. The Coordinated Services Outreach grant supports the project. It is funded by the New York State Department of Education, administered by the Department of Library Development. The contact person is Ellen Loughran, coordinator of the Public Service Support Office. Her telephone number is (718) 780-7779.

The last to be received is a Library Services and Construction Act project in Minnesota in the Southeastern Library Cooperating (SELCO) regional public library system. Individual inventories of member libraries were made and reported on, not only for accessibility for people with disabilities, but also for general overall condition. It was found that 60 percent of the facilities are accessible through ramps, elevators, or at-grade entrances.

Internally, there are the usual difficulties,

such as aisle width and placement of fixtures (i.e., water fountains, telephones, and the like). Restrooms provide the largest area of inconsistency. While 60 percent of the buildings are accessible, excluding restrooms, only 43 percent of the restrooms are accessible. Needed modifications range from the proper placement of mirrors to total reconstruction and fixturing.

In summation, nearly all of the facilities need minor modifications such as door hardware, exit sign location, possible illumination, and emergency lights, while six others need major reconstruction, such as door installation and exterior modifications for new exits. The contact person is Alan Lewis at (612) 296-2821.

There are many other examples of the "best" library programs throughout the United States. This is only a sampling.

I started with Robert Frost and shall end with an excerpt from his *Wild Grapes*.

> My brother did the climbing and at first
> Threw me down grapes to miss and scatter
> And have to hunt for in the sweet fern and hardhack
> Which gave him some time to himself to eat
> But not so much, perhaps, as a boy needed.
> So then to make me wholly self-supporting
> He climbed still higher and bent the tree to earth
> And put it in my hands to pick my own grapes.

DAVID ESQUITH: One of the most interesting things that came to my mind while Phyllis was giving her presentation was the snapshots at the end. Where is this money coming from to do some of these things? I hope at some point you all will be sharing information with each other about sources of funding for the kinds of adaptions and accommodations you have to make.

The other thing that struck me was what a wide range of things people are doing within their library and how you make decisions on where to begin. It must be a very difficult process to try to set priorities within your facilities.

There is a lot of talk about balanced budgets and spending. Certainly no one is talking about any more money. I think everyone is himself or herself for the size of the cut. Congress gave us this mandate, so where is the money to do something? I'm certain this must be a theme in a lot of your approaches, but creative funding is a critical issue. Probably you know best where you can get support for some of the work that you have to do.

Adaptive Technology to Access Information

Leonard Anderson

This presentation will center on the use of adaptive, or assistive, technology to access information. But I'm going to chase a couple of rabbits, if you allow me, and end the presentation with a series of slides of job site modifications that I call "what do you mean reasonable accommodation?" Even though these might be worksite adaptations that may or may not utilize high tech, low tech, no tech, bubble gum, or paper clip solutions, I hope that you can get some ideas from them on how this activity might be translated into areas within your library.

I want to mention again something noted this morning, and that is the booklet in your packet called "Surveying Public Libraries for the ADA." It has four authors, who are all mentioned on the front, and is an excellent work. I read most of it this morning. We do a lot of assessments and surveys of facilities to check for compliance for accessibility, and I have not seen a better work. With it, you can do your own assessment and avoid having to spend a lot of money for somebody to come in and do it for you. You decide how your compliance is going.

In this booklet there is a section on auxiliary aids and services that libraries can and must provide. Assistive devices are mentioned in this article. However, you won't find anything in the law that says these particular devices must be used— that is, a listing of particular devices is not there. And there is a very good reason for that.

What happens if five years from now the technology has outstripped what we have today and you have much better access through technology? The language of the law leaves room for the continuing invention of devices. What we should be aware of is that libraries are in a category in which some assistive devices must be provided because of the service and kind of services provided.

When we think of access to library materials, our thoughts go to those with sensory impairments. That is, persons who are blind or sight impaired, those who have hearing impairments or are perhaps deaf, and we sometimes carry that over into speech. Through my work over the past several years, I've learned that persons with physical disabilities have equal problems in accessing information, especially in a library setting. What happens when somebody maneuvers down the aisle between two stacks in a wheelchair and needs to reach something six feet off the floor? That's pretty difficult. It's somewhat the same problem as the blind person who cannot read the card file or a computer display.

A very simple solution to physical limitations is the use of reachers. Though this kind of thing is very low-cost technology, I'd like to just say a word that really probably shouldn't be part of my presentation. I think we have a speaker later who will address the issue of sensitivity to persons with disabilities. But, having worked in this area for about seventeen years now, I find that my best resource is the person with whom I am working, the person who has a disability and can tell me what to do.

I have a very good friend who is a Ph.D.—a college professor in engineering—who was in-

---

Leonard Anderson is Vice President of Technical Services, Rehabilitation Engineering Center, Wichita, Kansas.

jured in a fall and became a wheelchair user as a result. Because of this, now, when he goes to a restaurant, the waitperson will invariably ask his wife, "What does he want?" He is a Ph.D.; he speaks quite well for himself.

But for some reason when we see a person in a wheelchair or carrying a sensing device for the sight impaired so that they will know where they are and where they are going, we automatically assume that they are deaf as well. My friend says that everyone assumes he is deaf because they scream at the top of their lungs whenever they talk to him. Although when they turn to talk to his wife it's in a quite normal voice, he gets screamed at all the time. So sensitivity awareness is quite important in this business.

I'd like to say, too, that I think it's important to consider making your entire building and facility accessible, and not just a tech center as some libraries are doing. I think when you zero in on the establishment of a technical assistive device center within the library, you tend to lose sight of the need to make other areas accessible as well.

I come to you today because I gave a presentation at a statewide conference on the ADA that a number of librarians attended. Because of my presentation, I was asked to come and speak to you today. It so happened that our meeting was held in a room in a library. When I went to the restroom, it had the universal accessibility sign on the door, which means there is at least one stall or use area in the bathroom for a person in a wheelchair. When I went in I noticed there were two stalls: One of them had a couple of grab bars in it and was wide enough to get a chair in it with a person, but there was only one option for transfer, which was straight ahead—you couldn't turn the chair sideways. It's a rather awkward way to transfer, even though some people choose to do it that way. I pointed out to the meeting attendees that after the person had deposited himself on the business end of the stall, there sat the wheelchair, and he couldn't close the door on the stall. I suggested if you all want to do your thing for all to see, that's okay, but sometimes when we have the accessibility symbol out there, it doesn't mean everything is accessible.

When we talk about reasonable accommodation, there is no choice but for libraries to provide access to materials for persons with disabilities. The law says, and I think I'm quoting now, that plans for making specific areas of service delivery accessible to people with disabilities must include the provision of auxiliary aids and services. Again, there is no list of required aids and services. That's left open for future invention, and so we must stay current with technology.

There are many good examples of the assistive technology devices in the booklet on surveying libraries. I took a quick walk through the exhibit area after lunch. Many of the devices that I'm going to discuss are displayed there. Please avail yourself of the technology exhibit; you won't see just a slide of the devices and hear someone talk about them, you can have some hands-on use of the particular devices.

I'm not going to push or plug brand names today. There are several manufacturers of the devices that I'm going to show. The slides I have are pictures of particular manufacturers' devices, but I will simply just tell you what they do; I'm not here to sell anybody's products for them. Now for the slides.

Just a word about the discipline in which I practice, called rehabilitation engineering. In the early 1970s there was a movement in the Department of Education to establish centers that would perform research in the area of rehabilitation. The term *rehabilitation engineering* was coined then, although for some time prior to that we had seen engineers working with physicians in modifying the human body in several ways, vis-à-vis the artificial hip joint and heart pacemaker. Now we have artificial knees! Some are doing work on the back, using the engineering science applications that would be necessary in that area.

Since then, rehabilitation engineering has branched out into many areas. My particular area of focus for research is that of vocational rehabilitation. We look for ways to make work or job possibilities for persons with disabilities of all kinds.

As we go through the slides and look at some of this technology and the devices that are provided to assist us in accessing information, bear with me as I show them to you and tell you what they do.

This is the TDD—the telephone device for the deaf. You will notice the cradle on which you can lay the telephone receiver. The cradle can accomodate the handset of any telephone, and the person operating this device, which has a keyboard similar to that of a typewriter, simply types the message that he or she wants to send. The message appears digitally. As you see, it says "hello mother" in green-colored letters. The person using the device can tell if they have made an error. Whatever scrolls across the screen goes out over the telephone line and is received by a similar device at the other end, whether it's across town or long distance. Thus, with this device, two deaf persons can talk to each other, or a deaf person can talk to a hearing person using this device.

It was mentioned this morning that relay stations are now in place. I know we have at least one in Kansas. A deaf person can call the relay station, and an operator equipped with a TDD to receive the message can call a relay on to the deaf person they would like to contact, and through a relay system the message is conveyed.

So you don't have to have a TDD located everywhere. This technology is not high priced; there is one on display in the exhibit area— ask the attendant how much one costs.

We had a young man who is severely stricken with cerebral palsy and unable to speak at our place last week. He had a TDD with him, which he used to communicate with us. He could do a hunt-and-peck system with one finger. So he talked with us, that is, communicated with us with this device. One of these could be installed at your check-out desk, front desk, or other strategic location in the library, and in those cases where you have short-term communications with persons with hearing problems, you could use this very easily as a means to communicate. Also, pen and paper isn't too bad a way to go in most cases.

I want to introduce a thought that you should carry with you. It seems so simple that maybe it's trite to mention. Persons who have hearing difficulties, whether they simply have hearing loss or are deaf, need to receive input by sight or feel. So you use things like flashing lights to catch their attention. There are modules that plug into any 110-volt outlet in homes or businesses. You can plug an item like a light or lamp into the module, and connect it with the telephone as well so that when the phone rings the light flashes, indicating to the nonhearing person that the telephone is ringing. Even with a TDD, you wouldn't know the phone was ringing if you were unable to hear.

We also have emergency systems in buildings, such as fire alarms. With these, we need flashing lights, or strobe lights, something that will catch a person's attention, because people who cannot hear need input by sight.

Here is an example of the devices plugged into lamps, that sort of thing. Very simple installation and very low cost technology, probably on the order of much less than $100 per unit.

Here is an alarm clock for a person who cannot hear. The white square on the left end of this clock is a flashing light. I don't know if you have ever tried it before, but even if you are a very sound sleeper, if a light begins flashing in the room, you will wake up. It is an easy way to solve that problem.

Another way to give input to the nonhearing person is through other senses— touch, for instance. This happens to be an alarm that you put under your mattress and it vibrates to wake you up. Maybe some of us might even want it to go longer than just to wake us up!

Here is a very simple aid for persons with sight impairments. What can be done for those who have sight problems? Well, sight impairments range from what I have, even less than what I have (to the trifocal arrangement now). I'm a user of that assistive technology. A lot of us are users of assistive technology.

Here is a very simple device, a large magnifying glass on legs. You place it over books, maps, etc. At $9.95, this device (hand-held magnifier), is inexpensive enough to have a half-dozen sitting around the library. They would be very helpful.

This slide illustrates a real problem, and I think it helps us to begin thinking about problems for people who cannot see. This is a new product developed at the Smith Kettlewell Institute, which has been a rehabilitation engineering center funded by NIDRR for a number of years. Their principal area of work has been the development of devices that help people with sensory impairments.

What happens when a person who is blind takes out a TV dinner or gets a can off a shelf— are they going to open corn, beets, or pickles? So the problem is, what do I have? This is a brand-new technology. In the upper left-hand corner we see our blind friend has placed the TV dinner on a machine that looks much like a fax machine. But it has a different way of picking up the image. It uses what is called a telefax process. The fellow has laid the TV dinner on the reading portion of this sending unit. He is in San Francisco and has called his friend in Sacramento, who is receiving the image from the sending unit on her computer screen, and he asks, "Can you tell me what I have?" And she says, "Sure, Jay, you have Top Shelf tender beef roast on the fax machine. If you turn it over I will give you the cooking instructions." Even though he's hundreds of miles away from his friend, this fellow is able to get her assistance using this technology.

This device is in our device library. It is called a talking alarm clock. When you touch the black bar at the top of the triangle, the clock tells you what time it is, to the closest minute, with synthesized speech. You can also set the alarm on the clock, which is a rooster crowing. I think this device costs from $40 to $50.

There are all kinds of devices with synthesized speech. This is a pocket calculator that gives you voice feedback. With it, the nonsighted person can know what's happening on the calculator. Every time you push a button, it tells you which button you pushed. When you push a button for an operation, it tells you the answer that has been calculated.

We also have a wrist watch, about a quarter inch thick and one inch square, that uses synthesized speech. You push a button on the side of it and a little voice gives you the time to the nearest minute and lets you know if it's a.m. or p.m.

Here is a device that will take your blood glucose level and give you the results in synthesized speech.

Most libraries now have their card file on a computer-based system of some kind. For about $300 to $1,000, depending on what you want to spend and the quality you wish to purchase, you can add a speech-synthesis system to your existing computer by simply adding the circuit board shown here. This happens to be a particular brand, but there are many that do this. Then, on your existing computer, as you press certain keys on the keyboard, you get voice feedback. This is a means for persons who are blind to use the card file with existing technology, modified slightly.

This is a device that will convert printed text to synthesized speech. The Kurzweil reader is next door for you to see. This isn't the Kurzweil, but it does virtually the same thing. The device on the right is the reading device. You put your printed material upside-down on this. It scans it and turns it into digital information. This information is then displayed on the computer screen with the added advantage that all of that information can be stored on a disk. With one of these devices in a library, a person desiring information from a particular volume can lay the open volume on the reader, get it read, and then store it on disk. If that person has a personal computer at home with the same sort of software, he or she can take the disk home and have that information at home as well.

This is a hand-held scanner. You can scan a book by laying it open and moving the scanner over it. The scanner digitizes the information, stores it on disk, and displays it on the screen of a computer. After that, a synthesized speech output device on the computer can tell you the information that you have just scanned. By the way, this particular reader, I'm told, understands and will transpose hundreds of type styles. The function has been built right into the software.

This is just a computer setup that we have in our center, so that people can come try different technologies before they decide what to purchase. Here we see two different styles of keyboards: the standard one and another one that responds to a very soft touch. People who use a mouth stick can use that keyboard quite easily. You'll notice standing on edge something called a key guard. For people who have unsure hands— spasticity, that sort of thing— placing the key guard over the standard keyboard prevents a person from hitting two keys at a time. Their fingers go down through the holes in the key guard. There is a microphone in the center of the setup that provides voice-recognition capability. It demonstrates to folks how they can simply talk to the computer and have it register what they have said.

This is not the final word in technology. There are a lot of problems with the current voice-recognition technology. But we are getting close to the "Star Trek" routine where you talk to the computer and it talks back to you. On the top shelf of the setup is a voice-synthesis speaker that will convert any information displayed on the computer into speech.

This is a copier that makes braille copies. The copies it produces have raised portions on them. You can put a map on here, a map of California for instance, and it will produce a copy of that map with the roads and other features raised so that you can tell by feel what the map looks like.

I'm going to go quickly through some work sites. I want to give you an idea of the technology employed, both high tech and low tech.

This young lady is blind, She works at a Red Cross office as a receptionist, and is using a device that costs under $200. She handles eight incoming lines with fifteen staff people in the office. She simply needs to know which lines are ringing, on hold, or busy. She does that with the device she is holding in her hands, which is about the size of a ballpoint pen and which has a light sensor in the tip of it. It gives her audible feedback when it's passed over a light. If the light is blinking at a fast rate, the line is on hold. If the light is solid, the line is busy. This is the only piece of equipment that was purchased for this young lady to do her job. She has a sign on the front of her desk that says, "Hello, I'm blind. Please announce the staff person you would like to see." That was all there was to it.

Here is a guide for a blind person to place a rubber stamp on a job where the stamp is made on the same corner of every page. It's just a simple locating tool.

Here is another locating tool for a rubber stamp. Mount a self-inking stamp on a lever that locates the stamp. Place a document in the locating holder, lower the lever, and press the stamp. This makes this job available to people with poor hand function or sight impairment.

This is the back door to a Pizza Hut. A deaf person was working there. They wanted her to answer the rear door. We put a flashing blue light above the door that went off when the doorbell was pushed to let her know that someone was there. The manager thought this worked so well that he wanted her to be able to make pizzas. The area where they make pizzas has a printer that prints orders received from the front cash register. The hearing people know when an order comes back because the can hear the printer run. We went into the printer and tapped off of a place that provided power when the printer was running and put a red flashing light at the top of the menu board. Because this worked so well, there are now three deaf people working in the kitchen of that Pizza Hut.

Here is one we did with mirrors. The person operating this microfilm camera was too short to see the meter that was located on the top. The first mirror reflects the meter, with the image upside-down and backwards. The second mirror reflects the first mirror's image and turns it right-side-up and forward. The worker simply views the meter in the top mirror on the left.

A young man with an arm amputation wanted to work in a post office and couldn't handle sorting the mail with his prosthesis. By providing a simple holding tray, we allowed him to do so. He also had to put rubber bands around stacks of letters corresponding to a city block. That's tough to do with one hand. So we invented the device shown here, which we called the "one-handed rubber band putter-oner." It makes it easy to access the rubber band— drop it down and retrieve the stack of letters.

Lazy Susans are a great help. Here you have a lazy Susan within a lazy Susan. There is a lazy Susan bearing under the larger circular board on the bottom and a bearing under each of the three on top. We had a young lady starting kindergarten that didn't have arms; she simply had hands growing out of her shoulders— functional but with limited range of motion. The lazy Susan gave her access to crayons, scissors, pencils, the sorts of things she needed in school.

Here is an office set up for a lady with multiple sclerosis. The lazy Susan on the left end of her desk is one of the secrets to helping her. In this close-up, you can see the various things she has put on the lazy Susan that are quite easy to access; she can turn the surface easily with her limited strength.

In her filing system she had files that were not confidential, so rather than put them in four-drawer file cabinets that she couldn't access, we simply built tables that went around the periphery of her office. Her files were then held out open and easily accessed; she just pulls the one toward her she wants to look at.

She also had information in three-ring binders, for which we invented this device. It holds six three-ring binders hinged across the bottom edge. With very little strength or range of motion you can reach up and grab the top of the binder that you wish to get information from. It falls open then and is held in place. When you are finished you can close it with your two hands up and push it back into place. We made two of these in the first go-around. We just received an order to make two more for her.

Here is a device to help people who have poor use of their hands and cognitive problems to fold letters. In a mass mail-out of single-page letters, the whole stack can be set on this device; the top letter is folded about the platen shown here, and a perfectly folded letter is produced.

Here is a young man who was a machinist who lost the use of his right arm in an accident. He is running a machine that requires the use of two hands— one to hold the workpiece and one to push two buttons. To the left of his head are located push buttons. One is labeled "open," the other "closed." These buttons operate the powered chuck on the machine. We paralleled these buttons out into a bracket within which he places his head. The bracket has two padded stations, one on each side of his head, with microswitches. He moves his head to one side to produce the "open" function, and the other way to produce the "close" function of the chuck.

Here is a filing system for a young lady with

limited strength and range of motion. It is a personnel file and has to be lockable and fireproof. We put an elevator inside for the young lady. She had to access the equivalent of two four-drawer file cabinets. By running the elevator inside she exposes one shelf at a time. She then can retrieve the file using two simple tools that we made for her to access the files.

Here is a workstation we made for a young lady who received a severe whiplash injury in an automobile accident. Her physician wouldn't let her return to work unless she could be in a semireclined position with her head fully supported. That indicated "Lazy-Boy recliner" to me. We hit the local furniture store and bought one to fit her. By the way, she is transcribing court records using a computer in this setup. That's her job. Also, I'm taking orders for this workstation, if any of you are interested!

Here is an application to allow for change of elevation of about two to three feet. This happens to be a wheelchair lift that would normally be put in a van. The twelve-volt DC system uses a battery, of course. In the home it takes up little space on the floor and folds up in a place for safe keeping. It operates when the power is out because it run as long as the battery is charged.

Here is a workstation for a fellow in a wheelchair. He's operating a five-horsepower drill press. We simply lowered it down and canted it thirty degrees from the vertical, which gives him nice access to the throat of the machine and also utilizes help from gravity. When the operator gets the part close, it tends to fall in place.

In Kansas we have many folks on farms who are injured and who operate tractors with hand controls on brakes, clutches, etc. This fellow did this lift modification himself.

A young lady does all the tractor work on the farm. The husband would throw her over his shoulder, as she is rather small, carry her up on to the seat in the cab of the tractor, and go off and leave her. She wanted to be independent. So we fixed this lift device for her.

This is probably the most sophisticated job that we have people in wheelchairs doing. These are computer-controlled milling machines. This fellow is using a porch lift to get up to a platform that has been put in place for him so that he can access the working part of the machine.

ESQUITH: Thank you very much, Leonard. That was fascinating. I know one of the questions, as I'm sitting here watching all these fascinating and ingenious job accommodations, is, Where do I get some more information on materials like this or strategies for job accommodations? When we get to the Q & A period we will try to provide as many resources as we can, so when you have a specific question, you will have a few contacts to help you get some information.

Making ADA Work

Richard Sheppard

I must admit I'm a little nervous. Recently an acquaintance of mine who used to be a friend delivered a mortal blow to my speaking ego. He described me as a model speaker. Warm and mellow. You might think, What's wrong with that? Well, I felt pretty good about it until I went home and consulted Mr. Webster. And first, of course, I determined that "model" means a small imitation of the real thing. And then I went on with my consultation and learned, of course, that "warm" means not so hot. And then I went even further, and it appears that one definition of "mellow" means overly ripe and nearly rotten. So I hope you will bear with me this afternoon in my nervousness as we conduct this last session.

I would like for this to be a participatory session. I would like to make some comments and share with you a wonderful video, and then the rest of the session will be interactive.

This morning Mary Lou referred to the famous Harris poll that was conducted back in the sixties, and I'd like to elaborate a little on that poll. As Judy Herrmann said during lunch, things have gotten worse since the Harris poll in the sixties. The Harris poll defined a person with a disability in this society in one way: It said that you are unemployed if you happen to be disabled. And it said, as Mary Lou indicated, that two-thirds of all Americans with disabilities of working age, aged 60 to 64, are not working. And while actually less than one in three of us has a job, only one in four of us works full-time. There is no other population under 65 that has such a small percentage employed, including young black Americans.

If you happen to be black and have a disability, your chances of being in the labor market drop to less than one in five. Eighty-two percent of African-Americans of working age with disabilities are out of the job market.

It's an issue the President's Committee has been concerned about for some time, when we have gone to major cities throughout the country to start new strategies for involving minorities with disabilities in a more meaningful way in preparation to work and in getting jobs.

When they ask the participants in the Harris poll whether they preferred working to receiving some kind of support payment, well over two-thirds indicated that indeed they wanted to be out working rather than sitting at home watching the soaps. When asked the reasons they felt frozen out of the economic mainstream of our society, over 20 percent cited lack of assistive devices necessary to make them employable. Almost 30 percent blamed lack of accessible, affordable transportation. Approximately 40 percent indicated lack of education, training, and marketable skills. But well over 50 percent cited attitudinal barriers as the reason that they were not employed.

I would like at this point to share with you a wonderful video that has recently been released by Easter Seals with ADA about attitudes toward people with disabilities. It's called "Nobody Is Burning Wheelchairs." I don't get a

---

Richard Sheppard is Manager, Office of Plans, Projects, and Services, The President's Committee on Employment of People with Disabilities.

cut, but I encourage you to invest in the video—it's only $35 from Easter Seals in Chicago. I think it's really excellent.

We frequently talk about attitudinal barriers in a very vague way. We refer to biases and prejudice toward people with disabilities. I do three-hour workshops where we deal in depth with our own feelings about disability experiences and people with disabilities. We work on objectifying our feelings so they don't get in the way of the way we interact with people with disabilities. We are not going to have time, obviously, to do that this afternoon.

First, I would like to define an attitudinal barrier and give you some examples of the most common attitudinal barriers that we as people with disabilities experience. An attitudinal barrier is a way of thinking or feeling that results in behavior that limits the potential of people with disabilities to be independent.

Let me give you some examples of some of the more common attitudinal barriers faced every day by people with disabilities. One of the oldest ones—many of you in the audience will recognize this—is called *paternalism,* an overly protective attitude, a feeling that because one has a disability he or she is not competent to take care of himself/herself and cope effectively.

And I guess maternalism, since so many of you are ladies, is related to paternalism. It's appropriate for us to be kind in our interactions with people, but we have to guard against overextending feelings of kindness and protectiveness. Especially toward people with disabilities, because paternalism and maternalism carried too far have the ultimate effect of denying a person with a disability his or her independence and dignity.

Another example of a common attitudinal barrier is *focus on disability.* I have an example that I experienced this week. I have a friend who works for the President's Committee He is about six feet, three inches; uses an athletic chair; and is a very handsome Vietnam-era veteran. He's quite a contrast to me; I'm about five feet, seven inches, and use an electric cart. We won't go beyond that.

Anyway, I went into a restaurant that both of us have frequented right around the corner from the President's Committee and the waitress says, "I know what you are going to order." She immediately gave me the name of John's favorite drink.

She was so focused on my disability and that we both came in there that she somehow didn't individualize us, didn't recognize our differences. She just focused on the fact that we both happen to be disabled.

That happens to me all the time in our condominium, which has 225 units and where about five of us are tenants with disabilities. I have a friend named Rick who has cerebral palsy and weighs about 250 pounds and also uses a manual chair, and again I don't need to describe myself; we are frequently confused. He has light hair and no beard, by the way.

So sometimes people get so focused on the disability that they don't recognize the individual. That happens to disabled job applicants all the time, where the focus is on the disability rather than on the skills, talents, abilities, and education of the applicant. The employer or the interviewer frequently tends to go through the process of thinking, "Well, gee, these are the essential functions of the job, but I wonder whether he or she can really do this or that?" Again, the focus is too much on the disability.

Another common one is *fear of persons with disabilities.* Judy mentioned this at lunch. We all are fearful of becoming dysfunctional or disabled or ill. We share this common fear, but that's not what we are talking about here.

Dr. Robert Kleck has done extensive research into this area. We call it the "behavioral deficit theory," wherein nondisabled people think they really don't know how to act appropriately around people with disabilities. They are fearful of doing or saying the wrong thing and therefore offending a disabled person.

Kleck, in order to prove his point, for years has been putting people with disabilities and nondisabled people in a "first encounter" situation and studying their reactions. What he has noted over and over again is a sort of ambiguous reaction on the part of a nondisabled person that gives way to avoidance and then to definite signs of withdrawal from the situation.

What Kleck says is that all of us, nondisabled people as well as individuals with disabilities, need to learn "breakthrough" techniques—ways of breaking through that discomfort level. There are a number of breakthrough techniques that we could discuss; one is humor. In the video, Kathy Buckley certainly uses that well—dispels attitudinal barriers through the use of humor. Another one is what we do with everybody when we encounter them for the first time. We start exploring common interests. Use of one's first name is another way of setting up an opportunity for positive interaction.

Finally, *stereotyping* is an attitudinal barrier that we need to guard against. I come from the dark ages of rehabilitation; I can still remember if you happened to be blind and walked into a rehabilitation agency, they immediately tested your potential to be a piano tuner. There was a stereotype that all blind people were all naturally musical. All were considered potential piano tuners or perhaps even another Stevie Wonder, if they were very, very talented. The second thing they tested you for was to be a vending stand operator. Those were stereotypical ideas about what blind people could do in those days. Fortunately we have moved a long way from that.

If you happened to be hearing impaired or deaf and you went into an agency, they thought of you as a potential printer, because you could work in rooms where the excessive noise printers made wouldn't bother you. That's stereotypical thinking. Fortunately, we have left that far behind.

Stereotypes are still with us; they have become more subtle. We need to guard against them. I have heard over and over again what I consider to be "appropriate language" during this miniconference. We are now all using "people-first" language. We no longer talk about people as the deaf, we talk about people with hearing impairments. We no longer talk about people as the blind, we talk about people with visual impairments.

It's sometimes awkward language and we are getting a little more comfortable with that. We talk about deaf individuals and blind persons and so on. But please be sure to stick with "people first" language as much as you can as you work within the disability arena.

I've had an opportunity to conduct a great deal of awareness training for many, many managers and supervisors and many different groups. Library personnel happen to be one of those groups, and what I have done this afternoon is draw out some of the typical questions that have been asked in those sessions.

Do any of you know about "Windmills"? "Windmills" is wonderful attitudinal-awareness training. It consists of fourteen different modules designed to enhance our awareness and increase our sensitivity toward people with disabilities. This is one simple exercise of those fourteen called the "Ask It Basket," in which people write on a 3-by-5-inch card what they have always wanted to ask about people with disabilities or the disability experience but were afraid to ask. They write it down and then we reflect it back to the audience.

PARTICIPANT: What are some positive steps you can take to successfully integrate a new worker with a disability into your work force?

SHEPPARD: What are some positive steps? What have some of you done? None of you have ever had the experience of integrating staff?

PARTICIPANT: You ask about accommodation, what the new employee needs to function in the job.

SHEPPARD: What about the attitudes of coworkers? Do you deal with those or don't you deal with that issue? Has anybody in that situation had to do that?

PARTICIPANT: We have.

SHEPPARD: You explored a combination of things but you didn't do anything special beyond that. Does anybody else have something on how to integrate?

PARTICIPANT: We have a supervisor who has a staff that resents the fact that accommodation was made for a disabled employee. And he deals with it like he deals with all staff problems, if they're attitudinally based; essentially he tells complaining staff to grow up.

SHEPPARD: Any other techniques?

PARTICIPANT: We use the "People First" video from ALA to sensitize staff.

SHEPPARD: There is a new ALA video called "People First." And it's a tool that you may use. My own bias is that I'm against doing anything special when a new worker with a disability comes in. Some want to immediately go to staff and somehow make that worker special and unique by doing a special-awareness program about that person's disability. I think we need broad, generic education about people with disabilities. Any other responses to this?

PARTICIPANT: The most important thing is to set up communication for the disabled worker.

SHEPPARD: Especially with his coworkers and peers who work with him on a daily basis. Don't embarrass the person with a disability by inappropriately dealing with that. May we have another question?

PARTICIPANT: What is the best way to react to people who make negative, condescending comments about persons with disabilities?"

PARTICIPANT: Grow up.

SHEPPARD: Any other responses besides grow up?

PARTICIPANT: The same way that they would react to sexual comments or comments against minorities or anyone. You don't appreciate such comments.

PARTICIPANT: It's an opportunity to educate people. Frequently.

SHEPPARD: Other responses? A lot of times I ignore such comments.

PARTICIPANT: I would suggest giving the person a copy of *Disability Rag*.

SHEPPARD: I think that's an excellent solution. Any other reactions to that?

PARTICIPANT: On occasion I have parents who have kids who notice I'm different, and there are all kinds of questions.

Parents are embarrassed about their kids' reactions and they say to their kids, "Pretend it's not there." One wants the opportunity to explain to them what the disability is, to be forthright about it. That works better, don't you think?

SHEPPARD: Curiosity is very common. I know when I shop at the Giant Food Store, there will be a little kid who will point at me and say, "Mommy, what's wrong with him and why is he riding in that?" The mother will yank the child's arm out of the socket, creating a new person with a disability. What I always try to do is patiently and fully respond and try to make the mother and the child feel comfortable with the fact that I had polio when I was a child and I use this electric scooter as a way of getting around. It takes the place of my legs that don't work too well.

Again, I think that people with disabilities have a lot of responsibility for reacting in a positive way.

PARTICIPANT: A person with an apparent mental health problem approaches your desk and is very disruptive. What are your responsibilities?

SHEPPARD: This is something I'm sure that many of you face. How have you handled it?

PARTICIPANT: We have had this problem at our library. If there is no reference question and they are not using our library, we warn them several times that they are being too disruptive. Then we tell them to leave the library.

SHEPPARD: I don't know if any of you have the luxury of security staff, but sometimes it's necessary to involve them in getting rid of somebody who is disruptive. I think initially you owe the person an opportunity to see if they want some kind of meaningful service from you. That's your initial response. But if the person continues being disruptive, I think you have to protect the rights of the other clientele.

PARTICIPANT: What percentage of workers with disabilities requires accommodation, and what is the best way to decide on appropriate accommodations?

SHEPPARD: There is a common myth that virtually all workers with disabilities require reasonable accommodation in one form or another. There have been several studies about this, and actually less than 35 percent of workers with disabilities require any kind of accommodation. One of the major resources is the Job Accommodation Network, an excellent resource of the President's Committee on Employment of People with Disabilities. I'm not saying that as a plug; I'm simply saying that's what many of you have told us. Their number is 1-800-JAN-7234. There are brochures in the back, and I'm sure many of you picked up the Job Accommodation Network brochure. The system has over thirty thousand examples of accommodating workers with functional limitations—not only physical limitations, but mental impairments as well. I encourage you all to become familiar with the JAN system. There are other ways of also learning about accomodations.

PARTICIPANT: I would like to say that if someone has a disability and they are your worker, talk to them. Ask them how you can best accommodate them in doing their job.

SHEPPARD: That's the first step. Of course, after they understand the essential functions of the job, let them be involved in the process of accommodation. But if that doesn't resolve your questions, then JAN is an important resource and there are many other systems out there. But JAN has become one of the more important ones during the last eight years. I encourage you to call JAN and test it out.

We now have a 1-800 number: 1-800-ADA WORK. It's especially designed to respond to questions about ADA compliance. I believe that's also in your JAN brochure.

I brought with me a handout titled the "Ten Commandments of Etiquette for Communicating with Persons with Disabilities" (see appendix C). I encourage you to read through this and also to circulate it among your staff. These are excellent guidelines on communicating with people with a variety of disabilities and for answering the questions that the gentleman had in the video. What's the etiquette? This just came out about three weeks ago and we reprinted it for your benefit.

There are times when I think we have made tremendous progress in our understanding in our society of people with disabilities. And then there are other times when I'm not exactly sure. Let me give you an example.

Recently I was riding home listening to my car radio and I was tuned in to one of those programs where callers call in and get what's really bugging them off their chests— sort of a catharsis at the expense of the poor listener. A gentleman called in and identified himself as a senior citizen.

He said, "What's really bugging me, what really bothers me are these kids on skateboards." He went on and on venting his anger about these very inconsiderate young people who go barreling down the sidewalk paying absolutely no attention to their fellow citizens, particularly older people who may have mobility problems and have trouble getting out of the way.

At the end of his angry statement he said, "Now society is condoning the behavior of these inconsiderate young people." The announcer said, "What do you mean?"

"Now at the end of every block we have these cuts in the curbs so these kids can go from one block to another without even slowing down."

The announcer, being very good at his job, said, "Sir, you really don't understand. Those curb cuts are not for kids on skateboards. Those curb cuts are for disabled citizens." The elderly gentlemen paused and said, "That makes it worse because disabled citizens have no business on skateboards."

So sometimes I think we are gaining insight and then the clouds roll over again. I think, though, that if we can focus the positive energy and commitment that I have felt among you today, all of us— people with disabilities and librarians— can stay off skateboards.

Questions and Answers

Leonard Anderson, Mary Lou Breslin, David Esquith, Joseph Shubert, and John Wodach

ESQUITH: The next segment of our program involves our panel answering your questions. I'd like someone to keep track on how many times one of our panelists says, "Maybe—that depends on this situation or that situation." I'm certain that they will try to be as forthright as they can.

I will ask the question, and whoever has an answer, pipe up. When a question is addressed to a particular individual, I will indicate that.

If a sign is posted to indicate that library staff is available to assist upon request, does this constitute reasonable accommodation for services, or is more required?

WODACH: Looking at the wide range of ADA responsibilities, there are going to be more things that are required than just posting that sign.

For example, a person with a visual impairment wouldn't know what services are available there. If you dealt with regular users, you might have some way of letting them know what services are available. You might have materials available in braille or in some other way that told people what services are there. Clearly that is certainly a good first step.

You don't have to say to every person that comes in, "By the way, we have the following services." Posting the sign and having information available that can be handed to people as to what services you provide for persons with disabilities is a good first step, and then, of course, providing the service.

Is the library or the group using the library's meeting room responsible for communication access at the group's meeting? Meeting room use is free.

WODACH: The first issue to deal with here is whether we are talking about Title 2 or Title 3. To a certain extent if, under Title 2, the group is part of the program of the library, then the library has some responsibility. If we're talking about the library just making a room available to community groups for free, then it is the group's responsibility to deal with that.

Under Title 3 the answer may be somewhat different because of the way the act itself is written. You are a private library, and you are a public accommodation. You are responsible for auxiliary aids for all those things that go on in your facility, whether or not you are receiving funds for them.

In addition, the group that is using your library may itself have some obligations because they are an accommodation for themselves. So if a local day-care center is using your facility for its annual meeting, they would have an obligation to provide, say, sign language interpreters or some kind of auxiliary aid because they are a public accommodation. You, as a private entity, would also have that kind of obligation for what goes on in the library.

Keep in mind, though, there are a number of things that, especially if it's a free service, might have an impact on it. This is a true "it depends." And it depends on whether you are a public or private institution. It may seem a little unusual that in this case the private institution has a broader obligation than the public one; it's just the way the two laws have been developed.

Do newly purchased bookmobiles need to be equipped with lifts? The bookmobile is a library service outlet of the library and not the only point of library access available.

WODACH: This is rare—I'm going to answer with a yes or no. No. Library bookmobiles do not need to be equipped with lifts. The reason for that is there is a particular part of the ADA that says nothing in the ADA requires lifts on vehicles of this nature, taxi cabs, a whole range of other vehicles. However, the bookmobile services should be available. There are other obligations that go with providing the bookmobile service, even though the library system itself may have other ways of making its materials or its programs accessible.

So there may be things—for example, if there is kind of a bookmobile that people can go into it and look around at the displays, you may have some obligation in terms of the height of displays, the width of the aisles, if you have someone on crutches to navigate the steps into the vehicle who may be able to use them.

ESQUITH: Common sense would also dictate that if you are thinking about it, you would look to purchasing a bookmobile that may be accessible.

To what extent must the fifteen million people with mental illnesses be accommodated? Where is the line to be drawn in accommodating behavior symptomatic of mental illnesses? How can stigma and stereotyping be countered?

BRESLIN: If I had a couple of days I might be able to scratch the surface of that question. But the first part of the question that needs to be answered is to clarify who is covered under the ADA for purposes of the people with disabilities.

I want to make sure that everyone understands that people with mental and physical disabilities are covered under the act. That regardless of the type of disability that you have, if it is also a substantially limiting impairment, you are entitled to protection under the act.

The second two segments of the question are much harder because the answers will be very much fact specific. The correct answer is that when we are talking about providing an accommodation in an employment setting for a person with a psychiatric or mental disability, we are really talking about what might be appropriate to meet that individual's needs. The decision will be made based on what kinds of information are presented by that person; those who work in the facility might be able to provide the accommodation.

The question on stigma is a much broader one and I think it goes to a question of education and acceptance. I think that as a political statement about the issue, people with psychiatric histories and conditions are probably, among all of this, the most stigmatized and ostracized and by mainstream society. I think for most people it's very difficult to self-identify, it's very difficult to come forward and express needs and to have much empathy with respect to those needs once they are expressed. I would suggest that we need to look at our own biases and begin to determine what a person really needs to eliminate.

It's not a simple question or answer. I think it doesn't go much to more education than anything that we could talk about today.

WODACH: Title 2 provides protections to persons who are qualified individuals with a disability. The heart of this question may be, When someone is engaging in behavior that may be disruptive to what is going on in the library, what is it that you can or can't do?

It gets down to a question of whether the person is qualified to participate in the program that you have. If someone is really disruptive to the provision of services to other people in the library, then you can deal with that person's disruptions as you would any other person being disruptive.

Where you draw that line will depend. There may be a library in which anyone uttering any noise is evicted from the library. And therefore anyone falling within that rubric can be removed from the library, even though the noise may be the result of a provision that is covered by the ADA. It falls within that commonsense rule of reason. The ADA says you may have to think twice about things before you act on them and make sure that what you are doing is not discriminatory, but is based on the need to provide services in whatever the environment is that you are providing.

This issue comes up for a lot of providers of services. Restaurants, for example, would, and still do, evict people because their customers don't like seeing a person in a wheelchair, or there may be a person who drools when he eats. They don't want that person there. That would be discrimination on the basis of disability and a violation of the ADA. Someone who is disrupting the restaurant in another manner—making loud noises or going down the tables and disrupting other people—can be evicted from the restaurant for this behavior.

I think you have to come up with some rule concerning how you deal with these situations in your libraries. If you are in a small enough area where you are familiar with the customers that you are dealing with, you may find other ways to deal with persons who might want to avail themselves of the services that you have but might be disruptive to other clients. You might find a way to address that person's needs through your services in a way that doesn't impede the abilities of others to use your programs.

BRESLIN: Let me give a quick example of how that might work. We have a person working in our office who has a condition called Tourette's syndrome. This is a fairly rare condition but can result in involuntary articulations of noises and sounds and sometimes profanities, which can be incredibly disturbing and disconcerting. This is an involuntary condition— the person can't control the utterances— and I think that the point raised in this issue is just to remind you to do what John just said, step carefully when you are trying to make a decision about someone. Even if their behavior is disruptive, you might want to learn the origin of the problem and to look at whether there is some alternative way in which that person can participate in the program.

Perhaps move the person to a room where the behavior would not be disruptive to other people. I'm not suggesting that, if we have a terribly disruptive person that really needs to be dealt with, you don't have the right and the responsibility to do that. Do keep your mind open to the possibilities that some solutions can take a little bit of creativity, and not all situations may be what they seem to be.

Is a private agency that operates library services for a local government covered by Title 2 or Title 3? Local government gives money to private, nonprofit corporations to run the library.

WODACH: Oddly enough, this question comes up in a lot of different settings. It's one area that we didn't predict when we were doing the ADA— that there would be the wealth of multiple reasons that really exists in American society.

A private entity, the library in this hypothetical situation, has obligations under Title 3. The state agency or the local government, whatever is giving funds for this, has its own independent obligation under Title 2. Their obligations under Title 2 will be to make sure the entity, the private library they give funds to, is in compliance with whatever they have to do as a state agency.

This private entity might take on some additional obligations because of the obligation of the state action. Looking at it in a broad legal sense, if someone were going to sue one about this, they would sue the state agency under Title 2 of the local government— Title 2 violations— and go over to the library for the Title 3 obligations. So it's really an amalgam. In that situation, the library first operating independently just spoke to Title 3 obligations. The state, when it gives the money, might add something to it.

If there are four town libraries within five miles of one another but run independently— paid for by each town's taxpayers, have separate board of trustees— do the four town libraries separately need to meet all the standards, or can they be considered branches and only need to conform to the ADA as a group?

WODACH: They are considered separate and all must conform to the ADA. This situation is an old-line Section 504 ruling, and what tended to happen in the 1970s is that colleges wanted to know if they could form consortiums, which I think is at the heart of the question. Even though they were independent legal entities, "Come to a consortium, we have four branches of the state university, we make one of them fully accessible, we won't do things to the other three." That was not allowed under 504. That's a standard principle that's been put into ADA. Under Title 2 they are separate legal entities; each one has its own program accessibility obligation.

Are volunteers with disabilities covered under Title 1?

WODACH: We did training last week where this question came up. EEOC is the official entity that is the appropriate organization to answer that question. They had informed us, and this comes up in Title 7, that volunteers are not employees, that "employees" is a particularly defined term. When you are counting how many employees you have, if you want to get to fifteen or twenty-five or what obligations you have in an employment sense, volunteers are not numbered as employees.

Was there also some caveat about if the position the volunteer is moved to is a position of employment, was there a different—

WODACH: Not in terms of the employment obligations. Even though they are not an employee, as an entity that has obligations under Title 2, if you are operating a program with certain nondiscrimination provisions that are applying, even though not in an employment sense, you can't discriminate against volunteers on the basis of disability. It's not the employment part of that.

If an employee becomes disabled through a non-work-related situation, should the employer accept the employee's doctor's analysis, or can the employer require an employee to go to another doctor? In other words, who determines that the disability impairment really exists that requires reasonable accommodation?

WODACH: Starting at the end of that question, the employer certainly has to make these determinations, and it's not unreasonable for an employer to ask an employee in this situation for an independent analysis. It would be inappropriate for the employer to ask that person to pick up the tab and pay for it. It would be the employer's expense in that regard.

What often happens in these situations is you end up with dueling doctors. I guess I would caution that doctors often are not experts about employment—they are experts about medical situations. They may not often be experts on whether a person can perform the essential functions of the job, which is really something that the employer and the employee have to work out together.

But to get to the thrust of this question, an employer could do that. I would hope there would be some meeting of the minds. It is the employer's decision to make, to determine whether the person is entitled to the accommodation, but then if the employee disagrees, it sets in motion either a complaint or investigation of some kind.

I represent the library and the state-assisted university. As such, I understand we are covered by Title 2. When we contract for goods and services with entities as under Title 3, are we responsible for ensuring their ADA compliance or are they?

WODACH: This is sort of the reverse of a previous question. A public entity is always a public entity and is never covered by Title 3.

If a state library does contract with an entity that is a Title 3 private entity, its obligation is to ensure that its subcontractor is conforming. Let's assume that the contract for this private entity is to do some of what the public entity is required to do, library services. The state's obligation in that regard is to ensure that its contractors are operating in compliance with the state's obligations because the private entity is operating in the shoes of the state or the local government. Your public library has an obligation to ensure that your contractors are not discriminating on the basis of disability.

In addition, the contractor has its own obligations under Title 3 for which you are not responsible. You are only responsible for ensuring that for whatever the contract is about, that they are not operating in a way that will bring you in jeopardy under Title 3.

Is it fair to say as a general rule that if an entity has compliance responsibilities and they form a contract, subcontract out some work, this does not in any way reduce their compliance responsibilities?

WODACH: That's correct.

Do support groups for public libraries, such as Friends of the Library groups, need to make their newsletters, et cetera, available in nonprint formats if group members need this service?

WODACH: The answer to this question would depend on what the Friends of the Library are as a legal entity. If it's an arm, a part of the state agency, if it's part of your program, they have the obligation to make their program accessible—they have the obligation to provide auxiliary aids. So they may have an obligation here.

If it's an independent group that is not viewed as part of your program, then that may not be the case. In that case you might have to determine if Friends of the Library is a private organization that is a public accommodation and therefore has obligations.

I'm a member of the Friends of the Library for my local library. We have a newsletter and we do provide it in alternative format. I think we do that as matter of course. I don't think we have ever organized to see if we had the obligation under Title 2. The Friends of the Library organization that I'm familiar with is part of library services; it's an integral part of what the public library does and it has Title 2 obligation.

SHUBERT: I will add to that. It seems to me that that depends on the purpose of Friends. I can't imagine why a group would not want to do that.

WODACH: It may be due to cost. Braille may be difficult, but providing something on tape—having someone come and read the newsletter on tape, making that available—is probably a much better solution.

SHUBERT: There is opportunity to use the interest of other organizations and other levels of libraries to do braille noticing or taping. The regional library has equipment to do braille for all us. There are also community organizations such as the independent living center program, which has specialized resources. We would be glad to help.

Do any provisions of the ADA apply to persons with limited abilities to speak and understand English?

BRESLIN: Not being able to speak English is literacy, or viewed as such. It's not considered a disability under the ADA. Although the caveat is, if you used sign— exact English or another kind of sign English— and are not fluent in written and spoken English as a primary language, that would be considered an impaired condition. Not speaking English is not considered a disability.

Does the ADA cover individuals with environmental illnesses and their use of a library? What accommodations need to be made for such people?

WODACH: To answer this question you have to go back to what the statute says about who is covered. The statute says an individual with a disability is any person with a physical or mental impairment that substantially limits a major life activity. It's a functional definition. It is not a list of illnesses, diseases, conditions, or impairments that is included. Someone who has extreme chemical sensitivities would be covered by the statute and protected by the ADA if they have a major life activity that is impaired by this.

When we went through our hearing process for this, the issue was a particularly difficult one for us. The architectural and transit barriers compliance board has given some consideration to what this means. You have carpeting with formaldehyde in it and people are sensitive to that, does that mean you have to tear up the carpeting? Does that mean you have to instruct your staff not to wear certain perfumes? We have not said that any of these things are required by the ADA. There are no standards at the moment in the ADA for taking these issues completely into consideration.

It is clear that certain people will be protected. It's much less clear what you have to do. We have not said you have to put in new carpeting or that you have to create a scent-free environment; these things have not yet been required by the ADA.

BRESLIN: It's always hard when you are sitting next to the world's ranking expert on the ADA. I do think that as a clarification, the first question you want to ask regarding whether somebody is covered for purposes of the threshold test is, Are you covered as a person with a disability? A person might have a condition that's serious enough to substantially limit a major life activity like breathing; or perhaps other kinds of conditions come to mind. That person would technically be entitled to protection from discrimination under the ADA.

The next question that needs to be looked at is, What do you have to do? The regulations and analysis of the regulations, both with respect to Title 1, 2 and 3, basically say, "Don't give us any illustration of the ways accommodation might take form." It's important to remember that we have only a few examples.

People are going to be covered; and there is ongoing work on what kinds of accommodations or modifications might need to take place in order to make sure that the person has an equal opportunity to participate. So I hope you don't leave with the impression that we aren't covered as a general rule. Because, again, "it depends"; as it is with many of these issues, people rise to the level of "Are they going to be able to call for coverage under the statute?"

WODACH: Keep in mind that the ADA is fairly flexible and allows for creative solutions. With a situation in which you have someone who has difficulty breathing in the environment of your library, it may be that that's a situation where you can have a modification of your policy, and you can provide some way of delivering materials electronically or even bring materials to that person outside the library through bookmobiles or other services. That may work in some situations; it may not work in others. It depends on what's reasonable and whether it's a fundamental policy. That's very much the kind of thing that you will have to do on a case-by-case basis.

ESQUITH: I first came into contact with this issue about nine months ago as we were holding a long-range planning meeting in Berkeley and had someone call up and ask us to post signs outside the hearing room asking people not to wear perfumes or smoke. This is clearly, at least from my limited perspective, the issue that's moving east. By the time it hits Washington on a full-scale basis we may have different answers than we are giving now.

WODACH: I want to remind you that the EPA in Washington was forced to recarpet its entire facility because of contamination that resulted from the commercial carpeting in the building. It might have reached the East Coast.

Although the federal ADA employment guidelines apply to employers of twenty-five persons or less, and next year fifteen or less, individual states may have adopted narrower and more stringent guidelines. For example, the Kansas act against discrimination, which has been in effect for over two years, applies to employers of four or more persons. What's the relationship between ADA and state laws, which may have stricter requirements?

WODACH: It's a very good point and applies to not just the employment area but also the accessibility area in terms of constructing new buildings. Some states have more stringent requirements. So an employer that had five employees would have to be subject to the Kansas law in addition to any other. If the law had less stringent requirements, the ADA would command those if they provided for the situation. The rule of thumb is the stricter law is going to apply.

What is being done to assist or coordinate the production of alternate format information at all levels?

WODACH: This gives me an opportunity to promote a small program we have. We have nineteen grantees receiving a total of $2.4 million. One of the grants is to the National Center on Deafness and the Council of the Blind. The purpose of this grant is to provide information about development of alternative sources for the same kind of material. As materials become available under that grant, we will make them available.

In addition, the federal government is moving through several federal agencies to come to grips with making available a uniform policy for the provision of sources and materials in alternate formats, both in terms of what the policy is and how to comply with it. As we get that information, technical-assistance information, it's going to be available in a number of ways. The grantees, the disability business accommodation centers, have information in their booklets. They have telephone information services available on a regional basis.

Will there be more federal employees to assist with the complaints to agencies such as the EEOC?

WODACH: Usually people don't ask to have more people at the EEOC or the Department of Justice. I think there has been an effort at the federal level to add more resources to the enforcement and technical-assistance arms of the federal government dealing with the ADA. More people are being added both in my office at Justice and at EEOC.

It's a measure of the Bush administration's support for the ADA that positions and dollars have been added at a time when almost every other federal agency is experiencing cutbacks in money, services, and employees. There is some growth there both at the EEOC and at Justice. We have some money for technical-assistance grants; we are not sure that's going to make it through the process. We will have to watch and see what happens.

How are you going to let us know about the new technical-assistance materials being produced?

ESQUITH: I will again point out to you that the orange brochure in your pamphlet has nine or ten regional disability business technical-assistance centers listed in it (see appendix E). There is an 800 number that anyone in the country can dial to get to the technical-assistance center serving their region.

As director of those centers I'd like to give you my telephone number and encourage any of you to call me if you are having problems with any of these centers. My number is 202-732-5801. I really encourage you to use these centers. There is $3 million wrapped up in these ten centers to provide entities such as libraries with information, materials, technical assistance, and the opportunity for training, and to make referrals.

Congress has established a fairly well financed system of technical assistance through a number of agencies; the Department of Justice has done an excellent job of coordinating these technical-assistance efforts.

All the agencies who have technical-assistance responsibilities meet at least once a month to discuss and share materials and work out ways of getting materials distributed to entities like libraries. I encourage you to use any of these technical-assistance resources, and if you have problems with them, let us know so we can go back and tell the grantees that they need to improve their service delivery in one way or another.

ESQUITH: There is one text on where attitudes come from, titled *Images of the Disabled,* which talks about how the mass media have approached the issues surrounding persons with disabilities that really help to create, shape many of the attitudes that we have. I'm certain that there are texts—research on literature, history of literature, and shaping attitudes toward persons with disabilities—that could make a very positive program for libraries. As many of its users, particularly young users, run into texts where the images of persons with disabilities may be negative, it might be helpful to walk them through what those images are telling them and how to deal with those images. The Job Accommodation Network (JAN) is an excellent resource for questions about accommodations.

Leonard, would you like to identify any other resources that people can turn to similar to JAN?

ANDERSON: Yes. There is a network of the rehabilitation engineering centers throughout the United States—I believe there are eighteen such centers now. And we all have sort of a working relationship, so any one of us can be of help. I can personally be of help.

There is an organization called RESNA, which is the Association for the Advancement of Rehabilitation Technology. Within RESNA there are several special-interest groups. I happen to chair a group called the Job Accommodations Special Interest Group, and there are 150 members of that group who live all over the United States. We can make referrals for people who do job accommodations from that list.

Also, I wouldn't want to forget to mention again the Job Accommodations Network. I think virtually all of the workstations that we have done that are worthy of note have been reported to JAN and are included in their database.

The NIDRR network has a responsibility to publish and to tell what's going on in the area of research. We publish something called *Technical Briefs*; you are welcome to get on that mailing list and be notified of future issues as well as receive a publication listing past issues in these briefs. Those are some resources; there are many others.

ESQUITH: The ten NIDRR technical-assistance centers are being equipped with an electronic service directory that will allow the person who calls up looking for a particular product to automatically enter a very large database and identify the product's name, manufacturer, and a contact point. Use the NIDRR technical-assistance centers to get access to manufacturers' names, addresses, and telephone numbers for any products you might be looking for.

Which is preferred, "disabled" or "physically challenged"? This gets into some of the etiquette that we were talking about earlier.

BRESLIN: Many of you know there are preferred ways of referring to people with disabilities that need to be individualized in some places. "People who are physically challenged" and "disabled people" tend to be used. My personal preference, the one I think is becoming the most accepted standard of reference, is "people with disabilities." The reason that we ought to use that one is because it's the name of the major law that provides civil rights protection for the group. There are varying views on that subject, but that's my personal view.

In planning a new library facility, are there guidelines for the height that materials can be shelved? Do all materials need to be reached from a wheelchair, for example?

WODACH: If we are talking about any construction, the answer to that question is no. If you go to the ADA accessibility guidelines, there is a section in both UFAS—Uniform Federal Accessibility Standards—and the ADA Accessibility Guidelines. There are provisions there for the width; the minimum width between shelves is thirty-six inches. Although they suggest forty-two inches, what's required is thirty-six. There is no requirement for the height of the shelf. This is the same for all public accommodations—not just libraries, but grocery stores, and so on.

The world has not now been reduced in height to the standard reach ranges of persons in wheelchairs, which is why in libraries and in other areas it's important to have persons who may be able to assist—persons who can reach the top shelves to retrieve materials. But again, here the policy would probably be no different for a person in a wheelchair than for a person of short stature.

PARTICIPANT: There is one hot one: height limit in display, face-out display shelving such as a magazine rack. Otherwise there is none.

WODACH: There are also standards in terms of height for card catalogs. The minimum is eighteen inches; the maximum, forty-eight.

When a library has provided equipment or furniture to accommodate people with disabilities, should these stations be posted as such, even restricted for use to persons with disabilities?

WODACH: There is no requirement in the ADA for such things. We are talking about what's good policy. It's not a matter of what the law or the regulations are requiring. You may find different people with different points of view. My own personal preference would be not to do that. There are certain stations that clearly would be useable by some people and not others.

I think definitely the second part—identifying something is only for persons with disabilities—clearly runs afoul of the intent of the ADA. I think it's probably best just to not have any signage at all. Unless you are talking about libraries where there is a daily fight for the seats for persons with wheelchairs and those disadvantaged. Maybe others have a different perspective. There is nothing in the law that says one way or the other.

BRESLIN: I'm going to elaborate. Most of us have become used to seeing wheelchair-accessible bathroom stalls. One thing that made it possible for those stalls to be accepted in terms of new construction and alterations is that everybody can use them. That's a very attractive component in this integration.

What about videotapes that are not accessible to deaf users? Should libraries buy only films videos that have captions? And the follow-up question, Are vendors making captioned videos available?

WODACH: Well, if we go back to the ADA itself, it says that you must have effective communication with persons with disabilities.

If you rely fairly heavily on videotapes, then having them closed-captioned or open-captioned is something that you should consider. It's not the only way to make something accessible. There is no requirement that you replace videotapes that you would have in your library that people check out. If we are talking about materials that you would use in a training session, I think the requirement will be a little different.

More and more materials are being close-captioned. The federal government does not require closed captions, I think we are moving in that area. But there is no requirement for you to go back and redo everything, as there is no requirement that you have every book in your library available in braille.

Is it being done? More and more materials are being captioned; certainly materials that are done with federal funds must be captioned. Much of prime-time television is now captioned, and live events are being real-time captioned. One of the difficult issues we are facing right now is that we don't have a policy resolution on the marrying of state and local government requirements.

Cable television will tape the town meeting and just have cameras there. Is there a requirement for the town or the cable company to have captioning for the proceedings that are going on? That is something that we are struggling with in terms of what the requirement is, how much it costs, and what the legal responsibilities are in many areas between the cable companies and the town government.

How do copyright requirements impact on the need to alter print materials into other formats for people with disabilities?

WODACH: I certainly have no idea what the answer is. I looked at that as sort of a "stump-the-fed question"—it's something we will go back and look at. I know this issue came up with college professors' not wanting to allow students to tape their courses. That was solved by making the students sign waivers they wouldn't use the material that they got, especially when a professor was engaged in research. I think we need to look at copyright laws.

ESQUITH: If it turns out to be a barrier—it's quite a barrier getting things into alternate format, in terms of the extent to which materials are put in alternate format.

PARTICIPANT: At the School for the Blind in Maryland, we put things in braille. We also get a release from the publisher for those items going into braille. It's something that we automatically do and have done for a long time. Basically, there is no resistance from any of the publishers.

Did you get the sense that you had to get their permission to put it into braille?

PARTICIPANT: I can't answer that from a legal point of view. We feel from a safety point of view that it's very important that publishers are aware of what we are doing with their materials.

Do you or the publisher get the copyright for the braille edition?

PARTICIPANT: The School for the Blind, for example, when they are doing braille materials for a student, will write for a request release for that braille material. It's done directly with the publisher.

PARTICIPANT: I'm with the Illinois Regional Library for the Blind. The National Library Service provides us with thousands of books on a regular basis that are in adaptive format—recorded, braille—and the copyright is sought for every item. The copyright form itself was modified some time ago so there is a place for the holder of the copyright to check off that they will allow this material to be redone in adaptive format for those who no longer can read conventional material. This has been worked out for quite some time.

It is always appropriate for you, if you are doing this independently instead of through the National Library Service or American Printing House, two agencies that regulate clear copyright and educational material and recreational material, to contact the copyright holders for permission. It's also very rare for them to deny it.

How does scanning material and storing it on a disk relate to copyright law? Fair use isn't copying the whole book. What about a device like that?

ANDERSON: I rely on this analogy: There is an old automobile for which I don't have the owner's manual or repair manual, but there is one in our city library and they allow me to copy pages from that book for parts of the car that I need to work on. I would suspect that the scanning or changing to alternate format would be the same kind of thing. But perhaps not an entire volume. I would think if you can copy it on a photocopy machine, you could use a different kind of copy system. It would be worthwhile checking with a publisher on any issue that you have questions about.

ESQUITH: This is certainly a good example of an instance in which the field makes recommendations to people in the profession about how to handle a situation like this. You all are clearly experienced in this issue of copyright, and what's being presented here is that we have other ways of making copies.

If an addition to a library is built, does the rest of the original building have to be made accessible at the same time?

WODACH: Under a number of state laws the answer may be yes. This is one area where federal law is different from state law. It also depends on the size of the addition. You have to look at your state code and a number of other codes. If the addition is big enough, there is a requirement for creating an accessible route to the addition.

If you are doing an addition that doesn't have its own separate entrance, you may have to have an accessible entrance to it under state law. But under the ADA, under Title 2, you just have to make the addition accessible.

If you are talking about a private entity covered by the the alterations provision of the ADA Accessibility Guidelines, you have an additional obligation. Whenever you do an alteration that affects a primary function of the building or a major activity for which the building was intended, you have an additional obligation to create an accessible path of travel to the altered area, and to create accessible restrooms, drinking fountains, and telephones—in the words of the statutes—"to the extent it is not disproportionate in terms of cost and scope to the cost of the alterations." And that disproportional figure is 20 percent.

Basically, if you are a Title 3 private entity, you have to spend up to 20 percent of the cost on that alteration on accessible path of travel, which includes accessible restrooms and drinking fountains and telephones. It's probably the most complicated part of Title 3 issues because much of what gets figured into the 20 percent figure—of the altered area cost—is based on how do you do the computation. It's one of the areas where ADA leaves flexibility.

Before I came here I was at a convention in Seattle with the Building Owners Management Association. We spent two hours on an issue that's very important to them, because they said there is no new construction going on in the United States right now; it's all alteration work. They didn't want to know new construction requirements. For a Title 3 private entity there would be those obligations. For public entities it would depend on state and local building codes.

Are there guidelines for child-sized furniture and equipment, that is, tables that accommodate children with disabilities, and if so, where can we find them?

WODACH: There are none at the federal level. The Architectural and Transportation Barriers Compliance Board has identified this as an issue for which they are going to provide guidance. The ADA Accessibility Guidelines, UFAS, and most of the other existing accessibility standards are based on reach ranges, turning radiuses, and the size of a "standard" adult. There are several areas where there are no specific standards; recreation is one and facilities for children is another. There is research going on in this area and there will be standards, but not for the immediate future.

ANDERSON: There are guidelines for sizes to work with children. Dreyfus developed something called the Human Scale several years ago. It's used to develop furniture in schools for children of all ages and covers desk heights, table heights, those kinds of things for children. Wheelchairs, however, should be considered to be higher because the chair, by the nature of it, is higher than just the chairs children would use. So individual situations have to be looked at. The Dreyfus Human Scale is available from Massachusetts Institute of Technology. The last I heard they still are publishing it and have it available.

ESQUITH: We have time for one final question, and it's interesting to me that its subject, dealing with persons with mental illness, has been a recurring theme today.

We had an employee who was able to perform the essential functions of the position when hired. Over the course of time, however, mental illness has made him unable to perform without medication. The side effects of the medication make him a danger to coworkers. What are my rights and responsibilities as employer?

WODACH: The ADA and Section 504 and Section 503 and the whole range of federal laws that deal with nondiscrimination and disability in employment all talk about a person who is a qualified individual with a disability. If a person is no longer qualified to perform the essential functions of the job with reasonable accommodation to his or her disability, then he or she is not a qualified individual and can be fired in that situation. You have to look into the range of reasonable accommodations that might be available on a case-by-case basis. There are ways to ameliorate medication schedules with work schedules and look at that whole range of issues before you go to the step of firing someone. In cold reality, however, we are talking about someone who can no longer do the job, and the ADA is an equal-opportunity statute. If you had another employee who could no longer do the job for whatever reason, I assume you would fire that person and deal with the person with a disability in the same manner.

ESQUITH: That was our final question, and I would like to make a short observation. These have been excellent questions; they have shown an awful lot of thought and knowledge on your part of the ADA and issues that all of us, not just persons in library science, are now facing.

APPENDIX A

Self-Evaluation Survey for Public Libraries

Communicating and Interacting with Consumers with Disabilities

This Self-Evaluation Survey is reprinted with the permission of the State Library of Florida. It originally appeared in *Surveying Public Libraries for the ADA*, a cooperative publication of the Division of Library and Information Services of the Florida Department of State and the Pinellas Public Library Cooperative, and was written by J. B. Black, Janet Black, Ruth O'Donnell, and Jane Scheuerle in May 1992. Document development was funded under the provisions of the Library Services and Construction Act, as amended, administered by the State Library of Florida.

The Division of Library and Information Services, Florida Department of State reserves a royalty-free, nonexclusive, and irrevocable license to reproduce, publish, or otherwise use, and to authorize others to use, the copyright and rights of copyright for Chapter 7, *Surveying Public Libraries for the ADA*. Those rights are also retained by the federal government as authorized by 34 Code of Federal Regulations, Subtitle A.

Note: This survey is reproduced here in its original form, with pagination changed for its inclusion in this book.

GENERAL REGULATIONS FOR TITLE I: EMPLOYMENT

Surveying Public Libraries for the ADA

The following survey provides a self-evaluation for specific components of the Americans with Disabilities Act (ADA). The components included are accessibility, employment, public accommodations, auxiliary aids and services. This survey was developed for public libraries that are covered under Title II (Public Entities) of the ADA. Specifically addressed in this Survey will be Title I, Title II, and the Americans with Disabilities Act Accessibility Guidelines which affect public libraries. Although the survey has been developed to be as comprehensive and as thorough as possible, it is just one tool for libraries in their overall efforts to meet the requirements of ADA.

The ADA will have implications for all aspects of public library operations. Many of the items in this survey will need to be completed individually for each branch of the library and action taken will need to be individualized. This will ensure that all components of a public library have been included in the self-survey and that corrective plans will not exclude key components of library services.

The survey has been constructed so each question should be answered in the affirmative for compliance with the ADA. If an answer is no, then below each question a plan of corrective action should be developed indicating what should be done, who is responsible and time frames for the completion of each step. Additional space is provided to record progress concerning this plan of action.

If an answer to any question is yes, then the section concerning documentation should be completed. This documentation could include reference to library policy, date equipment was purchased, specific action taken or any of a variety of methods to document compliance. The completion of this survey and the accompanying corrective action will assist each public library to provide services which are available to all citizens.

58 Self-Evaluation Survey for Public Libraries - Title I

Title I Employment

1. Has the library staff **reviewed the following policies and procedures** to ensure that qualified individuals with disabilities have an **equal opportunity in employment**?

    Yes No
    ☐ ☐

    a. Recruitment, advertising, and job application procedures. ☐ ☐

    b. Hiring, upgrading, promoting, award of tenure, demotion, transfer, layoff, termination, right of return from layoff and rehiring. ☐ ☐

    c. Rates of pay or any other form of compensation and changes in compensation. ☐ ☐

    d. Job assignments, job classifications, organizational structures, position descriptions, lines of progression and seniority lists. ☐ ☐

    e. Leaves of absence, sick leave or any other leave. ☐ ☐

    f. Fringe benefits available by virtue of employment, whether or not administered by the library. ☐ ☐

    g. Selection and financial support for training including: apprenticeships, professional meetings, conferences and other related activities, and selection for leaves of absence to pursue training. ☐ ☐

    h. Activities sponsored by a covered entity including social and recreational programs. ☐ ☐

    i. Any other term, condition, or privilege of employment. ☐ ☐

    Action to be taken/Documentation

    Time Frame

    Progress

2. Does the library administration **make available equal employment opportunity notices, job notices,** job posting, training opportunities, employment rules, employee social events and other employee related material **in braille, audio tape, large print and announced in accessible areas?**

   Yes ☐ No ☐

   Action to be taken/Documentation

   Time Frame

   Progress

3. Are **procedures for requesting an interpreter** for the deaf or reader for the blind publicized on all job notices, job postings, tests, training opportunities and other employee related activities announcements?

   Yes ☐ No ☐

   Action to be taken/Documentation

   Time Frame

   Progress

4. Has the library staff **reviewed personnel rules and practices** to be sure that an applicant or employee who is a recovering **alcohol or drug abuser** (not currently using alcohol or drugs) **is not subject to discrimination?**

   Yes ☐ No ☐

   Action to be taken/Documentation

   Time Frame

   Progress

5. Has the library administration reviewed medical, hospital, accidental life insurance and retirement **fringe benefits to ensure** that they give **equal treatment** to people with disabilities?

   Yes ☐   No ☐

   Action to be taken/Documentation

   Time Frame

   Progress

6. Has the library administration established a **grievance procedure** that incorporates due process standards and that provides for the prompt and equitable resolution of complaints of discrimination including job applicants, employees, library users and visitors?

   Yes ☐   No ☐

   Action to be taken/Documentation

   Time Frame

   Progress

7. Have library staff ensured that **publications include notices of non discrimination?**

   Yes ☐   No ☐

   Action to be taken/Documentation

   Time Frame

   Progress

8. Has the library staff ensured that the library **does not limit, segregate or classify a job applicant or employee** in a way that adversely affects his or her employment opportunities or status on the basis of disability?

   Yes ☐   No ☐

   Action to be taken/Documentation

   Time Frame

   Progress

9. Has the library staff **reviewed contracts** and any other agreement or relationship with an entity to ensure that there is **not any affect of discrimination** for qualified library job applicants or employees with a disability?

   Yes ☐   No ☐

   Action to be taken/Documentation

   Time Frame

   Progress

62 Self-Evaluation Survey for Public Libraries - Title I

10. Has the above standard been considered for:

		Yes	No

    a. union contracts
    b. use of employment referral agencies
    c. use of temporary employment agencies
    d. provider of health care, pre-paid legal insurance or other benefits
    e. use of employee training seminars, conferences, workshops etc.
    f. use of apprenticeship programs

    Action to be taken/Documentation

    Time Frame

    Progress

11. Does the library **include in all its contracts** for personnel services a clause allowing for making **reasonable accommodations** for job applicants and employees with disabilities in the testing, training, selection, retention, and performance of the jobs.

    Yes   No
    ☐   ☐

    Action to be taken/Documentation

    Time Frame

    Progress

12. Has the library staff reviewed its **employment practices** to make sure that it is not using **standards, criteria** or **methods of administration which are not job related** and that perpetuate the discrimination of others who are subject to common administrative control?

    Yes ☐ No ☐

    Action to be taken/Documentation

    Time Frame

    Progress

13. Has staff **documented the need for each standard, criteria or method of administration** to an essential job function for every job classification.

    Yes ☐ No ☐

    Action to be taken/Documentation

    Time Frame

    Progress

14. Has the library taken steps to ensure that qualified job applicants or employees who are known to have a family, business, social, or other **relationship or association with an individual with a disability** are not excluded or otherwise denied a job or job benefits because of that relationship?

    Yes ☐ No ☐

    Action to be taken/Documentation

    Time Frame

    Progress

15. Has the library staff reviewed the **requirements of its jobs** (job descriptions, employment tests, or other selection criteria) to be sure that **no criteria are included that would discriminate** against an individual with a disability unless such criteria are job related and consistent with business necessity?

    Yes ☐ No ☐

    Action to be taken/Documentation

    Time Frame

    Progress

16. Has the library made **reasonable accommodations** to the known physical or mental limitations of an otherwise qualified applicant or employee with a disability, and if not has the library demonstrated that the accommodation would impose an undue hardship on the operation of that library?

    Yes ☐ No ☐

    Action to be taken/Documentation

    Time Frame

    Progress

17. Has the library administration developed a **process and procedure for determining reasonable accommodation** and is this available in writing and audio tape for employees and job applicants?

    Yes ☐ No ☐

    Action to be taken/Documentation

    Time Frame

    Progress

18. Does the above policy indicate that the **individual is not required to accept the accommodation**, but if they do not and can not perform the essential functions of the job they will not be considered qualified for that position?

    Yes ☐ No ☐

    Action to be taken/Documentation

    Time Frame

    Progress

19. Does this policy involve an **interactive process with the qualified individual** with a disability to determine potential accommodations?

    Yes ☐ No ☐

    Action to be taken/Documentation

    Time Frame

    Progress

20. Is the library staff prepared to make the following **reasonable accommodations** upon the request of an applicant or employee? | Yes | No |

   a. renovating existing facilities so they conform with the accessibility standards?
   b. job-restructuring; part-time or modified schedules; reassignment to a vacant position?
   c. acquisition or modification of equipment or devices?
   d. appropriate adjustment or modifications of examinations, training materials or policies?
   e. the provision of qualified readers or interpreters?

   Action to be taken/Documentation

   Time Frame

   Progress

21. Does the library have a policy to develop **reasonable accommodations** or adjustments to enable employees with a disability to enjoy the same **benefits and privileges of employment** as are enjoyed by other similarly situated employees without disabilities? | Yes | No |

   Action to be taken/Documentation

   Time Frame

   Progress

22. Does the library have a **procedure to document decisions** not to hire or promote because of undue hardship?

    Yes ☐ No ☐

    Action to be taken/Documentation

    Time Frame

    Progress

24. Has library staff **documented the relationship of each item** in a job description, employment test or other selection criteria to an essential job function for every job classification?

    Yes ☐ No ☐

    Action to be taken/Documentation

    Time Frame

    Progress

25. Has agency staff **reviewed hiring procedures** (applying, testing, and interviewing) for a job to ensure they are carried out in locations meeting the accessibility standards and are using accessible formats such as a reader/braille, audio cassette, written materials and sign language interpreters?

    Yes ☐ No ☐

    Action to be taken/Documentation

    Time Frame

    Progress

26. Has library staff **reviewed employment tests** to ensure that test results accurately reflect the skills or aptitudes necessary to perform the job rather than reflect the impaired sensory, manual or speaking skill of the applicant unless that skill is a critical element of the job?

    Yes ☐   No ☐

    Action to be taken/Documentation

    Time Frame

    Progress

27. Does the library have **a policy** with disciplinary action for any **supervisor or employee who retaliates or coerces**, intimidates, threatens or interferes, with any individual in the exercise of their rights under this act or encourages any other individual to exercise their rights under this act?

    Yes ☐   No ☐

    Action to be taken/Documentation

    Time Frame

    Progress

28. Has the library administration developed **policies and procedures that do not allow pre-employment medical examinations,** ask job applicants if they have a disability or ask job applicants if they have filed a worker's compensation claim?

    Yes ☐   No ☐

    Action to be taken/Documentation

    Time Frame

    Progress

29. Has the library administration ensured that any **medical examinations** or inquires as to the nature and severity of disabilities are made <u>after</u> **the offer of employment** is made and only if <u>all</u> entering employees in that job category are subjected to the examination regardless of disability?

    Yes ☐   No ☐

    Action to be taken/Documentation

    Time Frame

    Progress

30. Has the library administration developed procedures to maintain **separate and confidential files** regarding the medical condition or history of any employee with restricted access to only informing:

    Yes ☐   No ☐

    Supervisors and managers regarding necessary restrictions
    Accommodations on the work or duties of the employee
    First aid and safety, when appropriate
    Government officials investigating compliance

    Action to be taken/Documentation

    Time Frame

    Progress

Self-Evaluation Survey for Public Libraries - Title I

31. Does the library staff maintain on **file the reasons a job applicant is rejected** and why reasonable accommodations would not have overcome the limitations uncovered during their examination?

    Yes ☐ No ☐

    Action to be taken/Documentation

    Time Frame

    Progress

REGULATION REFERENCES FOR THE
SELF EVALUATION SURVEY FOR PUBLIC LIBRARIES

Title I

1. Regulation 29 CFR 1630.4
2. Regulation 29 CFR 1630.4
3. Regulation 29 CFR 1630.4
4. Regulation 29 CFR 1630.4
5. Regulation 29 CFR 1630.4
6. Regulation 29 CFR 1630.4
7. Regulation 29 CFR 1630.4
8. Regulation 29 CFR 1630.4
9. Regulation 29 CFR 1630.5
10. Regulation 29 CFR 1630.6
11. Regulation 29 CFR 1630.6
12. Regulation 29 CFR 1630.6
13. Regulation 29 CFR 1630.7
14. Regulation 29 CFR 1630.7
15. Regulation 29 CFR 1630.8
26. Regulation 29 CFR 1630.10
17. Regulation 29 CFR 1630.9
18. Regulation 29 CFR 1630.9
19. Regulation 29 CFR 1630.9
20. Regulation 29 CFR 1630.9
21. Regulation 29 CFR 1630.9
22. Regulation 29 CFR 1630.9
23. Regulation 29 CFR 1630.9
24. Regulation 29 CFR 1630.10
25. Regulation 29 CFR 1630.11
26. Regulation 29 CFR 1630.11
27. Regulation 29 CFR 1630.12
28. Regulation 29 CFR 1630.13
29. Regulation 29 CFR 1630.14
30. Regulation 29 CFR 1630.14
31. Regulation 29 CFR 1630.14

GENERAL REGULATIONS FOR TITLE II PUBLIC ENTITIES

General Regulations for Title II Public Entities

Self Evaluation

1. Has the library staff **with the assistance of individuals with disabilities evaluated current services, policies and practices** and determined aspects that may not meet the requirements of ADA regulations and modified these services, policies and practices?

   Yes ☐ No ☐

   Action to be taken/Documentation

   Time Frame

   Progress

2. Does the library plan to **maintain on file**, for public inspection, until January 25, 1995:

   Yes ☐ No ☐

   a. the list of persons consulted in performing the above activities; ☐ ☐

   b. a description of areas examined/problems identified; and ☐ ☐

   c. a description of any modification made? ☐ ☐

   Action to be taken/Documentation

   Time Frame

   Progress

Self-Evaluation Survey for Public Libraries - Title II

Notice

3. Has the library **notified users in the most appropriate manner** that it **does not discriminate** on the basis of disabilities?

   Yes ☐   No ☐

   This notification may be done through handbooks, manuals, pamphlets, posters, or other media methods, and must be available in accessible formats.

   Action to be taken/Documentation

   Time Frame

   Progress

4. Does the library provide **information to individuals with disabilities concerning accessible services**, activities and facilities and is this available in accessible formats?

   Yes ☐   No ☐

   Action to be taken/Documentation

   Time Frame

   Progress

ADA Coordinator

5. **Has an employee been designated as the responsible individual to coordinate** ADA compliancy activities and has the name, office, address and telephone number of this employee been made available to all interested individuals?

    Yes ☐ No ☐

    Action to be taken/Documentation

    Time Frame

    Progress

Grievance Procedures

6. Has the library **adopted and published grievance procedures** to resolve library users complaints of discrimination?

    Yes ☐ No ☐

    Action to be taken/Documentation

    Time Frame

    Progress

Non-Discriminatory Practice

7. Has the library staff made **reasonable modifications in policies**, practices, or procedures where necessary to avoid discrimination on the basis of disability, unless the library can demonstrate that making the modifications would fundamentally alter the nature of the services? The following policies, practices, and procedures should be reviewed to see if reasonable modification is needed to accommodate the needs of persons with disabilities.

   All public service procedures; Staff-to-public interaction practices; Communication practices; Planning, goal setting and budgeting practices; and, Other practices as individuals with disabilities request accommodation.

   Action to be taken/Documentation

   Yes ☐   No ☐

   Time Frame

   Progress

8. Are **procedures established** for determining reasonable modifications?

   Yes ☐   No ☐

   Action to be taken/Documentation

   Time Frame

   Progress

9. Has the library administered services, programs, and activities in the **most integrated settings** and provided separate services for people with disabilities only when such action is necessary to provide services that are as effective as those provided to others?

   Yes ☐ No ☐

   Action to be taken/Documentation

   Time Frame

   Progress

10. Does the library provide **services to persons with disabilities that afford equal opportunity to obtain the same result**, to gain the same benefit or to reach the same level of achievement as that provided to others? Service areas that should be reviewed to determine if equal service is available to people with disabilities include:

    Yes ☐ No ☐

    Registration; circulation; catalog of library materials, whether print or automated; interlibrary loan; information and reference; adult services programs; youth services and programs; media services; use of material and equipment restricted to in-library use; outreach/extension services; all library service outlets; and other services available in your library.

    Action to be taken/Documentation

    Time Frame

    Progress

11. Does the library **avoid imposing or applying eligibility criteria** that tend to screen out an individual or class of individuals with disabilities from fully and equally enjoying any service, program, or activity unless the criteria has been shown to be necessary for the provision of the service, program or activity?

    Yes ☐ No ☐

    Action to be taken/Documentation

    Time Frame

    Progress

12. The library **does not place a surcharge** on a particular individual with a disability or any group of individuals with disabilities to cover the costs of measures, such as the provision of auxiliary aids or program accessibility, that are required to be provided to that individual or group by the ADA?

    Yes ☐ No ☐

    Action to be taken/Documentation

    Time Frame

    Progress

13. The library **does not unnecessarily impose requirements or burdens on individuals** with disabilities that are not placed on others?   Yes ☐   No ☐

    Action to be taken/Documentation

    Time Frame

    Progress

14. The library **does not exclude or deny equal services**, programs or activities to an individual or entity, **because of an association or relationship** with another individual who is known to have a disability.   Yes ☐   No ☐

    Action to be taken/Documentation

    Time Frame

    Progress

15. Does the library provide individuals with disabilities the opportunity to participate as a member of its **advisory or governing board?**   Yes ☐   No ☐

    Action to be taken/Documentation

    Time Frame

    Progress

80 Self-Evaluation Survey for Public Libraries - Title II

16. Does the library in its **contractual or other arrangements**, utilize criteria or methods of administration that ensure an equal opportunity for individuals with disabilities to participate in all the programs, services and activities of the library? Example: use of meeting rooms.

    Yes ☐ No ☐

    Action to be taken/Documentation

    Time Frame

    Progress

17. Does the library **avoid perpetuating the discrimination of another public entity?** Example: the school system.

    Yes ☐ No ☐

    Action to be taken/Documentation

    Time Frame

    Progress

18. The library, in the **selection of a procurement contractor**, does not use criteria that subject individuals with disabilities to discrimination on the basis of disability.

    Yes ☐ No ☐

    Action to be taken/Documentation

    Time Frame

    Progress

19. The library **does not discriminate on the basis of illegal use of drugs** against an individual who is not engaging in current illegal use of drugs and who:

    Yes No
    ☐   ☐

a. has successfully completed a supervised drug rehabilitation program or has otherwise been rehabilitated successfully;

    ☐   ☐

b. is participating in a supervised rehabilitation program; or

    ☐   ☐

c. is erroneously regarded as engaging in such use.

    ☐   ☐

Action to be taken/Documentation

Time Frame

Progress

20. Does the library **maintain in operable working condition** those features of **facilities and equipment** that are required by the ADA to be readily accessible to and usable by persons with disabilities and is a record of this maintenance maintained?

    Yes No
    ☐   ☐

Action to be taken/Documentation

Time Frame

Progress

21. Are **accessible routes periodically checked** to make sure that they have not been obstructed?

    Yes ☐ No ☐

    Action to be taken/Documentation

    Time Frame

    Progress

22. The library **does not discriminate against any individual because that individual has opposed any act or practice made unlawful by the ADA** or because that individual made a charge, testified, assisted, or participated in any manner in an investigation, proceeding, or hearing under the ADA. The library has not coerced, intimidated, threatened, or interfered with any individual in the exercise or enjoyment of, or on account of his or her having aided or encouraged any other individual in the exercise or enjoyment of, any right granted or protected by the ADA.

    Yes ☐ No ☐

    Action to be taken/Documentation

    Time Frame

    Progress

23a. The library **does not deny qualified persons with disabilities the benefits** of or exclude them from participation in programs or activities **because the library's facilities are inaccessible to or unusable** by individuals with disabilities. Refer to self-survey section on accessibility in this document.

Yes   No
☐   ☐

Action to be taken/Documentation

Time Frame

Progress

23b. If a library is not readily accessible, has a **transition plan** for program access **been developed** with the participation of individuals with disabilities setting forth the steps necessary to complete such changes?

Yes   No
☐   ☐

Action to be taken/Documentation

Time Frame

Progress

84   Self-Evaluation Survey for Public Libraries - Title II

23c. Is a copy of this transition plan **available for public inspection?**

     Yes ☐ No ☐

Action to be taken/Documentation

Time Frame

Progress

23d. Does the transition plan:

    Yes No

1. identify **physical obstacles** that limit the accessibility of programs or activities to individuals with disabilities;   ☐ ☐

2. describe in detail the **methods** that will be used to make the facilities accessible;   ☐ ☐

3. specify the **schedule** for taking the steps necessary to achieve compliance and if the time period is longer than one year, identify steps that will be taken in the transition year;   ☐ ☐

4. identify the **official responsible** for implementation of the plan.   ☐ ☐

Action to be taken/Documentation

Time Frame

Progress

24. Has the library taken appropriate steps to ensure that **communications with users with disabilities are as effective** as communications with others? Are both printed and spoken communications accessible, either through auxiliary aids or alternate formats? Some examples are: Assistive listening devices at reference, information and circulation points for individuals who are hard of hearing; written information available in large print, audio recorded or braille format for people who have vision loss (applications, brochures, announcements, overdue notices, policies about services, etc.); adaptive communication equipment or services such as note writing for short exchanges, sign language interpretation for longer, more complex exchanges or programs, and electronic communication devices; public address announcement accompanied by a visual warning; TDD or equally effective telecommunication system for information provided over the phone; and, closed captioned video public service announcements.

Yes No
☐   ☐

Action to be taken/Documentation

Time Frame

Progress

25. Does the library provide, or have available, when appropriate, the following **auxiliary aids**:

    qualified interpreters
    note takers
    transcription services
    written materials
    telephone handset amplifiers
    assistive listening devices
    closed caption decoders
    open and closed captioning
    telecommunication devices for the deaf (TDDs)
    video text displays
    taped texts
    audio recordings
    braille materials
    qualified readers
    large print materials
    computer screen readers
    print magnification devices
    other aids and services to make library services accessible?

    Action to be taken/Documentation

    Time Frame

    Progress

Yes No
☐   ☐

26. Does the library provide for the **modification of equipment** or devices when necessary to meet the individual needs of people with disabilities? For example, is existing equipment modified as needed, such as changing an automated catalog station keyboard to large print keys?

    Yes ☐ No ☐

    Action to be taken/Documentation

    Time Frame

    Progress

Self-Evaluation Survey for Public Libraries - Title II

REGULATION REFERENCES FOR THE
SELF-EVALUATION SURVEY FOR PUBLIC LIBRARIES

Title II

1. Regulation 28 CFR 35.105
2. Regulation 28 CFR 35.105
3. Regulation 28 CFR 35.106
4. Regulation 28 CFR 35.163
5. Regulation 28 CFR 35.107
6. Regulation 28 CFR 35.107
7. Regulation 28 CFR 35.130
8. Regulation 28 CFR 35.130
9. Regulation 28 CFR 35.130
10. Regulation 28 CFR 35.130
11. Regulation 28 CFR 35.130
12. Regulation 28 CFR 35.130
13. Regulation 28 CFR 35.130
14. Regulation 28 CFR 35.130
15. Regulation 28 CFR 35.130
16. Regulation 28 CFR 35.130
17. Regulation 28 CFR 35.130
18. Regulation 28 CFR 35.130
19. Regulation 28 CFR 35.131
20. Regulation 28 CFR 35.133
21. Regulation 28 CFR 35.133
22. Regulation 28 CFR 35.134
23. Regulation 28 CFR 35.149
    a. Regulation 28 CFR 35.150
    b. Regulation 28 CFR 35.150
    c. Regulation 28 CFR 35.150
    d. Regulation 28 CFR 35.150

24. Regulation 28 CFR 35.160 and .161, also Title IV Section 402 Closed Caption requirements.
25. Regulation 28 CFR 35.160
26. Regulation 28 CFR 35.130

COMMUNICATING AND INTERACTING WITH CONSUMERS WITH DISABILITIES

90 Self-Evaluation Survey for Public Libraries - Consumers

1. Does the library have a staff organizational plan to facilitate use of services for users with disabilities? For example, is a staff member designated to monitor services to individuals with disabilities? Is a staff member designated to maintain expertise in the acquisition and use of auxillary aids, assistive devices and special materials?
   (Suggested; not a regulation)

   Yes ☐ No ☐

   Action to be taken/Documentation

   Time Frame

   Progress

2. Does the library have a mechanism for users with disabilities to evaluate services?

   Yes ☐ No ☐

   Action to be taken/Documentation

   Time Frame

   Progress

3. Does the library have a mechanism for advocacy groups for library users with disabilities to evaluate library services?
   (Suggested; not a regulation)

   Yes ☐ No ☐

   Action to be taken/Documentation

   Time Frame

   Progress

4. Does the library consider suggestions and recommendations by users with disabilities and work toward accommodating their special needs?

   Yes ☐ No ☐

   Action to be taken/Documentation

   Time Frame

   Progress

5. Does the library have a means to provide feedback to users with disabilities in relation to their comments and suggestions concerning services and programs at the library?

   Yes No
   ☐ ☐

   Action to be taken/Documentation

   Time Frame

   Progress

6. Does the library have an established policy to monitor interaction and decision-making among library personnel (staff and management) to assure that such interaction and decision-making reflects a philosophy that emphasizes the importance of services to all users of the library including individuals who have disabilities?
   (Suggested; not a regulation)

   Yes No
   ☐ ☐

   Action to be taken/Documentation

   Time Frame

   Progress

7. Does the library include in the annual performance evaluation of employees an assessment of attitude and performance skills displayed while working with individuals with disabilities?
   (Suggested; not a regulation)

   Yes No
   ☐ ☐

   Action to be taken/Documentation

   Time Frame

   Progress

8. Does the library have a method to assess the need of its personnel to develop or be reminded of appropriate attitudes and skills for serving individuals with disabilities?
   (Suggested; not a regulation)

   Yes No
   ☐ ☐

   Action to be taken/Documentation

   Time Frame

   Progress

Self-Evaluation Survey for Public Libraries - Consumers

9. Does the library provide training programs for staff to review and renew interpersonal communication skills with individual library users who have disabilities and with advocates of library users who have disabilities?

    Yes ☐ No ☐

    Action to be taken/Documentation

    Time Frame

    Progress

10. Does the library evaluate user satisfaction with outcomes of personnel training in information, acceptance and positive attitudes related to providing services and materials to users who have disabilities? (Suggested; not a regulation)

    Yes ☐ No ☐

    Action to be taken/Documentation

    Time Frame

    Progress

ACCESSIBILITY GUIDELINES

Self-Evaluation Survey for Public Libraries - ADAAG

Accessibility Guidelines Survey

IMPORTANT:

This checklist is designed for you to gain a better understanding of your library and the ADA Accessibility Guidelines for Buildings and Facilities (ADAAG). Use this section of the survey to locate areas which need improvement, but work with an architect or contractor to plan structural changes. Be sure you and the architect or contractor both have a copy of the ADAAG before you sign any agreement for work. Please ask questions and seek help if you are unsure about making changes in your library.

To get copies of the ADA Accessibility Guidelines call the Architecture and Transportation Barriers Compliance Board

    800 USA-ABLE   Voice or TDD
    800-872-2253

The ADAAG is also in the Federal Registrar. Please note that **Title II libraries can follow UFAS (Uniform Federal Accessibility Standards) or the ADAAG** until such time as a single standard for public entities is published. The UFAS is available from:

Architectural and Transportation Barriers Compliance Board
1331 F Street N., Suite 1000
Washington, DC 20004-1111
800-USA-ABLE

The ADA requirements became effective on:

- January 26, 1992, generally.

- August 26, 1990, for purchase or lease of new vehicles that are required to be accessible.

- Structural changes which are undertaken to comply with ADA are to be completed within three years of January 26, 1992.

- New construction for public entities that commenced January 26, 1992 must be in compliance.

Surveying Public Libraries for the ADA

Introduction

The American with Disabilities Act (ADA) requires that physical barriers in existing library outlets must be removed, except where to do so would result in a **fundamental alteration** in the nature of the program or in **undue financial and administrative burdens**. If barriers are not removed, alternative methods of providing the services must be offered. The title II, Public Services, regulations discuss a concept for the removal of physical barriers called Program Accessibility. See Sub-part D, Section 35.149 of those regulations for more information.

Getting Started

You'll need the following:

- tape measure
- yard stick or ruler
- carpenters level
- an assistant

The level needs to be the large size with a center bubble. The longer the level, the better and more accurate. Three or four feet is good. You do not need the most expensive level to do the job. **The proper use of the level will be explained in the section on curbs.**

Working with someone will help you to complete the evaluation in less time and the individual can provide additional comments and suggestions. You can take turns measuring and filling out the evaluation. By working in pairs, you will have two people who have assessed the building and should changes be required there will be two employees to ask questions and work with the architect and/or builder/contractor.

Also be sure to make positive comments as well as noting where improvements need to be made. Your comments, good and bad will help other staff to understand the ADAA Guidelines and how they affect the library.

Please note that there some questions or entire sections (such as the section on Passenger Loading Zones) that may not apply to you or your library. Therefore, you will have some questions unanswered and blank spaces in the survey. Please write not applicable in these sections. In addition, you may want to make copies of the survey if you have separate buildings or branch libraries. Using colored paper to copy on will help keep the surveys for different buildings in order. Also, when you evaluate ramps, stairs and handrails, and restrooms you can copy the sections to survey all ramps, stairs and handrails, and the men's and women's restrooms. If your building has more than one floor you'll need additional copies to survey the restrooms.

Where to start?

The first, and highest priority should be getting people into the building. If there are stairs on the exterior leading to the main entrance, is there an alternate accessible route or entrance? Are entrance doors accessible?

The following is a suggested list of priorities for possible changes to meet ADAAG standards:

- Install or improve exterior ramps and walks
- Install curb cuts and accessible parking
- Widen doorways and install accessible door hardware
- Make restrooms and other interior amenities (drinking fountains, elevators, etc.) accessible
- Make service counters accessible
- Lower shelves and widen aisles
- Arrange tables and seating in common areas and meeting rooms to assure clear paths of travel
- Install signs for doors and accessible areas within the library

Surveying Public Libraries for the ADA

Getting into the Library

Parking [4.6 in the ADAAG]

1. Are accessible parking spaces:

    - at least 96 inches (8 ft.) wide?
    - have access aisles between parking spaces 60 inches in width and part of an accessible route? **Note:** Two accessible parking spaces can share a common access aisle.
    - have a designated sign showing the symbol of accessibility?

    Yes No
    ☐   ☐
    ☐   ☐
    ☐   ☐

    Action to be taken/Documentation

    Time Frame

    Progress

2. Is one in every eight accessible parking spaces, but not less than one overall, served by an access aisle 96 inches (8 ft.) in width with signage which indicates "Van Accessible" under the accessibility symbol? **Note:** The use of "Universal Parking Design" (see appendix A4.6.4 of the ADAAG) will eliminate the need for a separate "van accessible" space and signage for "van accessible" spaces.

    Yes No
    ☐   ☐

    Please see drawing on the next page.

    Action to be taken/Documentation

    Time Frame

    Progress

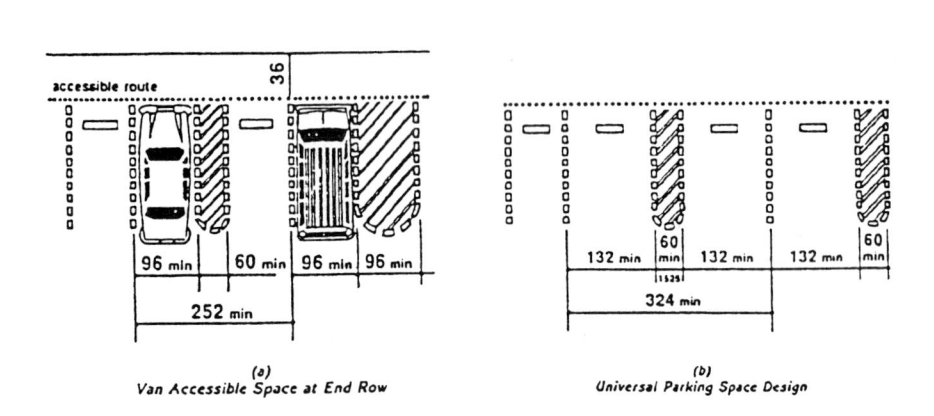

98 Self-Evaluation Survey for Public Libraries - ADAAG

(a) Van Accessible Space at End Row

(b) Universal Parking Space Design

3. Are accessible parking spaces located on the shortest accessible route of travel to an accessible entrance?

Yes ☐   No ☐

Action to be taken/Documentation

Time Frame

Progress

4. Do you have the required minimum numbers of accessible parking spaces? See Chart:

Total parking in lot	Required Minimum Number of Accessible Spaces
1 to 25	1
26 to 50	2
51 to 75	3
76 to 100	4
101 to 150	5
151 to 200	6
201 to 300	7
301 to 400	8
401 to 500	9
501 to 1000	2 percent of total
1001 & over	20 plus 1 for each 100 over 1000

Yes ☐   No ☐

Action to be taken/Documentation

Time Frame

Progress

Passenger Loading Zones [4.6.6]--(Drop-off/pick-up area for people adjacent to the library)

5. If your library has a passenger loading zone, does the zone have an access aisle 60 inches in width and 20 ft long, adjacent and parallel to vehicle pull-up space?

Yes ☐   No ☐

Action to be taken/Documentation

Time Frame

Progress

6. Are there any curbs between the access aisle and the vehicle pull-up space, if so, are there curb cuts or curb ramps?

   Yes ☐ No ☐

   Action to be taken/Documentation

   Time Frame

   Progress

Curb Cuts/Curb Ramps [4.7]

To use your level, you'll first need to mark some inch measurements. If the level has none, use masking tape on the top of the level and then write with a permanent marker at 10 in, 12 in, 20 in, 24 in, 25 in, and 36 in marks. Place the level long ways in the direction of travel. Slowly lift the low end of level until the center bubble is between the markings. With the ruler, measure the height of the bottom edge of the level to the ramp surface. Curb cuts, curb ramps and ramps are to have a slope of 1:12 or less. If you have a 3 ft level, the end of the level should be 3 inches or less from the ramp. (If the slope is greater than 1:12, you need to make changes in the curb cuts, curb ramp or ramps.) In addition, the sides of curb cuts and curb ramps (where they slope to meet the road or ground) are to be sloped to a ratio of 1:10.

7. Are there curb cuts or curb ramps at all curbs and walks on accessible routes to accessible entrances? **Note:** If you need to have curb cuts or curb ramps built, be sure you consult with someone knowledgeable about storm water run-off. You don't want to create an area which traps rainwater.

   Yes ☐ No ☐

   Action to be taken/Documentation

   Time Frame

   Progress

8. Do curb cuts or curb ramps have a slope of 1:12 or less and flared sides with a slope of 1:10?

   Yes ☐   No ☐

   Action to be taken/Documentation

   Time Frame

   Progress

9. If you have curb ramps. are they built so they do not extend into vehicle traffic lanes?

   Yes ☐   No ☐

   Action to be taken/Documentation

   Time Frame

   Progress

10. Are curb cuts or curb ramps 36 inches wide excluding the flared sides?

    Yes ☐   No ☐

    Action to be taken/Documentation

    Time Frame

    Progress

Please see the drawings on the next page.

(a) Flared Sides

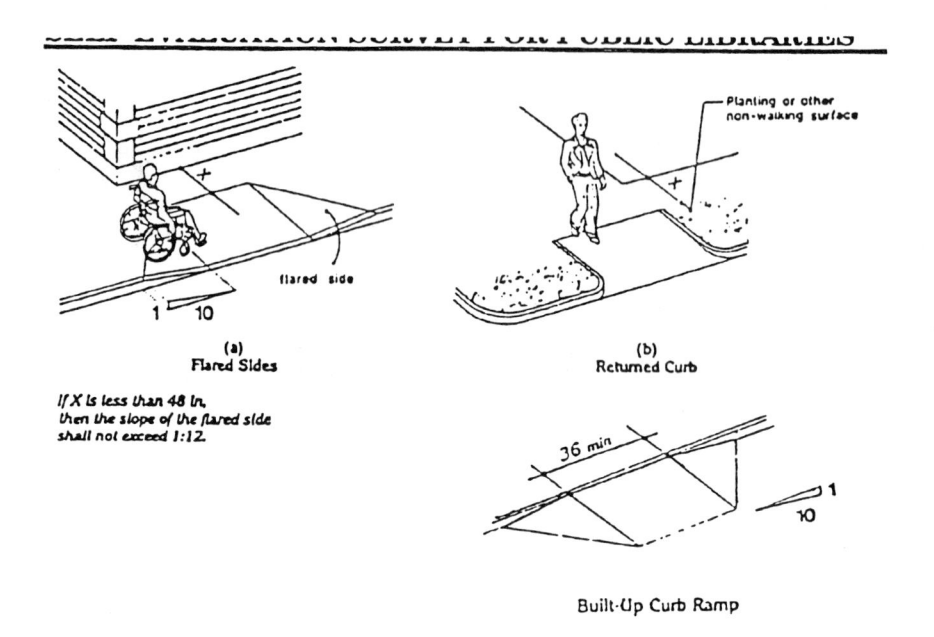

If X is less than 48 in, then the slope of the flared side shall not exceed 1:12.

(b) Returned Curb

Built-Up Curb Ramp

Ramps [4.8]

IMPORTANT

You will need to make copies of the section of ramps, stairs and handrails for all your ramps, stairs and handrails. Remember to include interior ramps, stairs and their handrails. Any part of an accessible route (outside or inside a building) with a slope greater than 1:20 is considered a ramp. The least possible slope should be used for all ramps. **Note:** In existing buildings or facilities where space limitations prohibit the use of a 1:12 slope or less for ramps, a slope of 1:10 and 1:12 is allowed for a maximum rise of 6 inches. A slope of 1:8 and 1:10 is allowed for a maximum rise of 3 inches. A slope steeper than 1:8 is not allowed.

11. Is the slope of all exterior walkways 1:12 or less?

    Action to be taken/Documentation

    Yes ☐   No ☐

    Time Frame

    Progress

12. Do the ramps:

	Yes	No
• have a minimum clear width of 36 inches?	☐	☐
• have level landings at the top and bottom, at least as wide as the ramp?	☐	☐
• have landings at least 60 inches in length?	☐	☐

Action to be taken/Documentation

Time Frame

Progress

13. If the ramp changes direction, is the landing at least 60 inches x 60 inches?   Yes ☐   No ☐

Action to be taken/Documentation

Time Frame

Progress

104 Self-Evaluation Survey for Public Libraries - ADAAG

14. If the slope of the ramp is:

    - between 1:12 and 1:16 does the ramp have a level landing 60 inches in length at 30 foot intervals?

Yes	No
☐	☐

    - between 1:16 and 1:20, does the ramp have level landings 60 inches in length at 40 foot intervals?

Yes	No
☐	☐

Action to be taken/Documentation

Time Frame

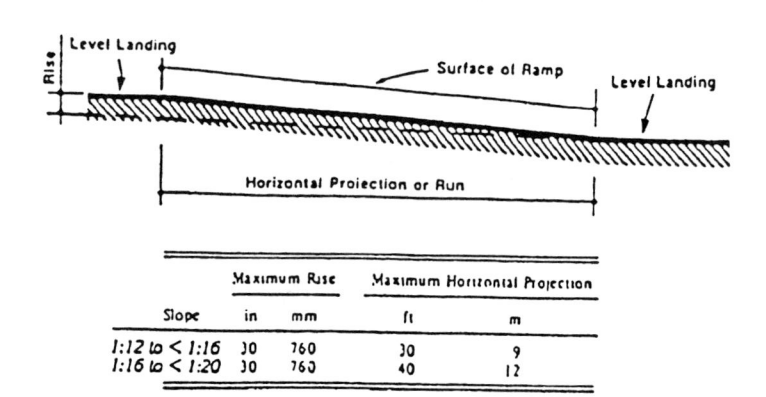

Progress

Slope	Maximum Rise in	Maximum Rise mm	Maximum Horizontal Projection ft	Maximum Horizontal Projection m
1:12 to < 1:16	30	760	30	9
1:16 to < 1:20	30	760	40	12

15. All ramps and walks are to have a cross slope of 1:50 or less and be designed so that water will not accumulate on the walking surface. To check the cross slope, place the level crossways on the walk, lift the level until the center bubble is between the marks. At 25 inches from the end measure the distance from the bottom of the level to the surface of the ramp. The distance should be ½ inch or less.

    Is the cross slope of all ramps and walks 1:50 or less?

    Yes ☐ No ☐

    Action to be taken/Documentation

    Time Frame

    Progress

16. If the ramp:

    - has a rise (a height) of 6 inches or more, does the ramp have handrails on both sides?

      Yes ☐ No ☐

    - is 72 inches (6 ft) or more in length, does the ramp have handrails on both sides?

      ☐ ☐

    Action to be taken/Documentation

    Time Frame

    Progress

Stairs [4.9]

Note: Stairs do not have to be eliminated, but accessible routes provided where there are stairs.

17. Are stairs at least 36 inches in width,

    - with all the steps on any given flight of stairs uniform in height and depth?

    - with step depths no less than 11 inches?

    Action to be taken/Documentation

    Time Frame

    Progress

18. Are the nosings (end of the steps) rounded or curved?

    - Do the nosings project no more than 1½ inches past the riser of the step?

    Please see the drawing on the next page.

    Action to be taken/Documentation

    Time Frame

    Progress

Yes No ☐ ☐ (×3)

Yes No ☐ ☐ (×2)

(a) Flush Riser (b) Angled Nosing (c) Rounded Nosing

Usable Tread Width and Examples of Acceptable Nosings

19. Do stairways have handrails on both sides?

    Action to be taken/Documentation

    Yes No
    ☐   ☐

    Time Frame

    Progress

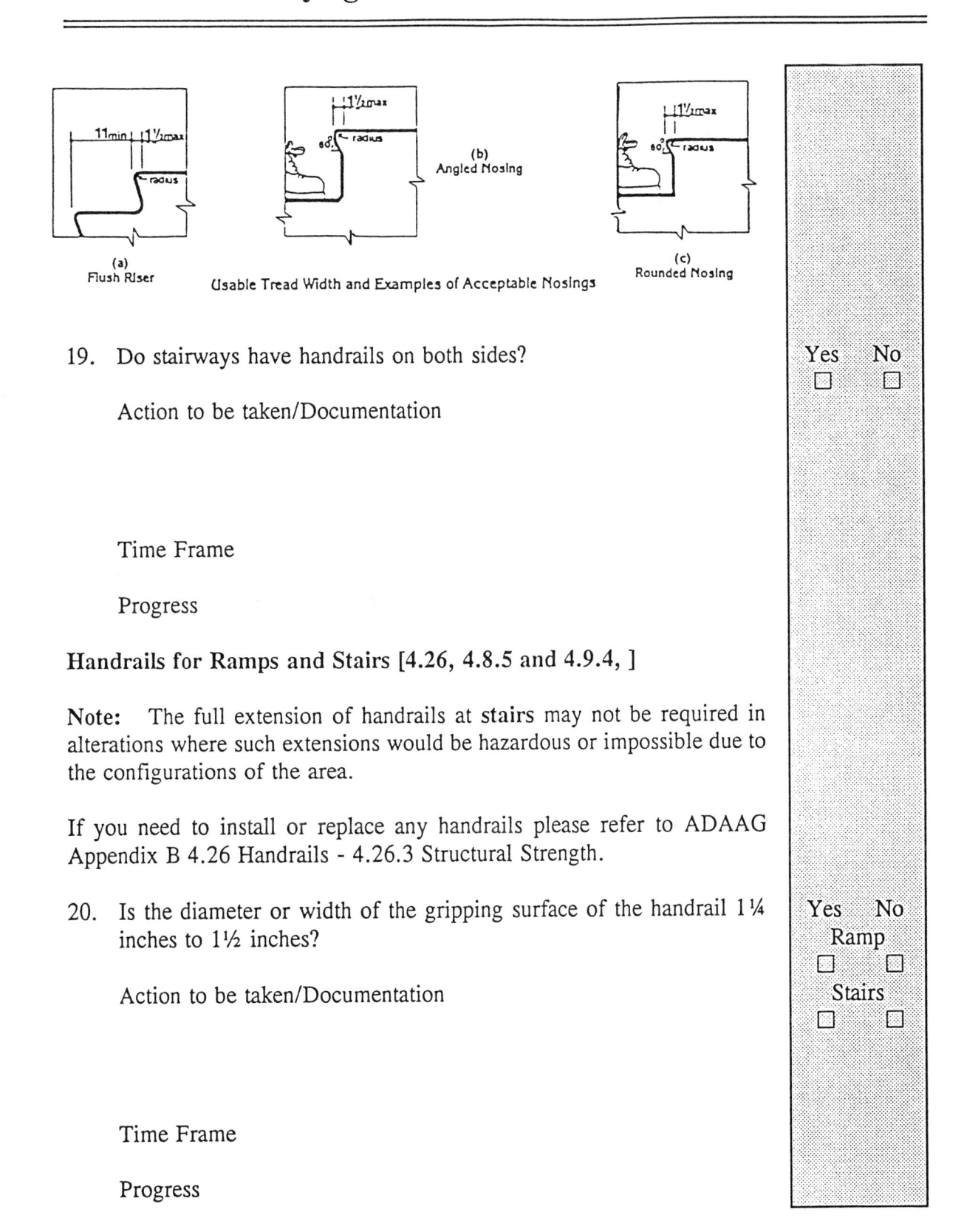

Handrails for Ramps and Stairs [4.26, 4.8.5 and 4.9.4,]

Note: The full extension of handrails at stairs may not be required in alterations where such extensions would be hazardous or impossible due to the configurations of the area.

If you need to install or replace any handrails please refer to ADAAG Appendix B 4.26 Handrails - 4.26.3 Structural Strength.

20. Is the diameter or width of the gripping surface of the handrail 1¼ inches to 1½ inches?

    Action to be taken/Documentation

    Yes No
    Ramp
    ☐   ☐
    Stairs
    ☐   ☐

    Time Frame

    Progress

108 Self-Evaluation Survey for Public Libraries - ADAAG

21. If the handrail is located adjacent to a wall, is the space between the handrail and wall at least 1½ inches?

    Action to be taken/Documentation

    Time Frame

    Progress

    Yes No
    Ramp
    ☐ ☐
    Stairs
    ☐ ☐

    (a) Handrail
    (b) Handrail
    (c) Handrail

22. If the ramp or stairs has a change of direction, is the inside handrail continuous?

    Action to be taken/Documentation

    Time Frame

    Progress

    Yes No
    Ramp
    ☐ ☐
    Stairs
    ☐ ☐

23. Does the handrail extend at least 12 inches beyond the top step for **stairs**, and 12 inches beyond the top and bottom for **ramps**?

    Action to be taken/Documentation

    Time Frame

    Progress

Yes   No
Ramp
☐   ☐
Stairs
☐   ☐

24. Are the extended sections parallel to the surface of the landing for **ramps** and the floor for the top step of **stairs**?

    Action to be taken/Documentation

    Time Frame

    Progress

Yes   No
Ramp
☐   ☐
Stairs
☐   ☐

25. Does the handrail extend the depth of one tread plus 12 inches past the bottom step for **stairs**?

    Action to be taken/Documentation

    Time Frame

    Progress

Yes   No
Stairs
☐   ☐

26. Does the handrail extension for **stairs** slope with the bottom step for the distance of one tread depth and is the additional 12 inches horizontal with the floor?

　　　Yes　No
　　　Stairs
　　　☐　　☐

    Action to be taken/Documentation

    Time Frame

    Progress

27. Is the top of the handrail gripping surface between 34 inches and 38 inches above the ramps or steps? **Note:** A second rail 10 to 12 inches below the top rail will be helpful to children.

　　　Yes　No
　　　Ramp
　　　☐　　☐
　　　Stairs
　　　☐　　☐

    Action to be taken/Documentation

    Time Frame

    Progress

Surveying Public Libraries for the ADA 111

28. Are the ends of handrails for ramps and stairs:

    • rounded or return smoothly to the floor or landing?
    • secure in their fittings (not allowed to rotate within their fittings)?

    Action to be taken/Documentation

    Time Frame

    Progress

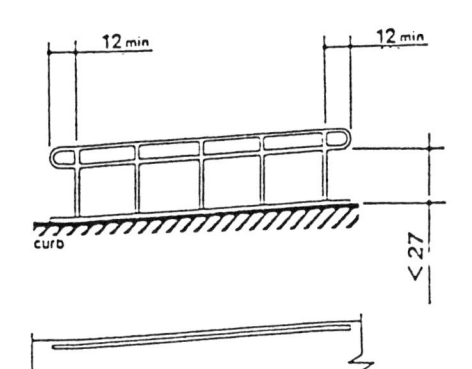

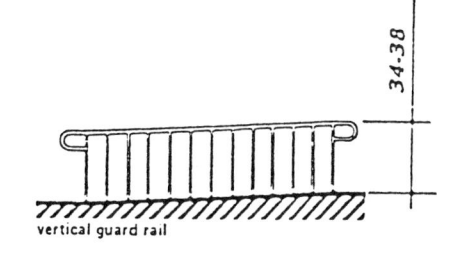

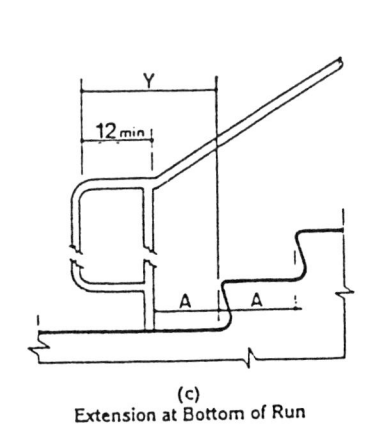

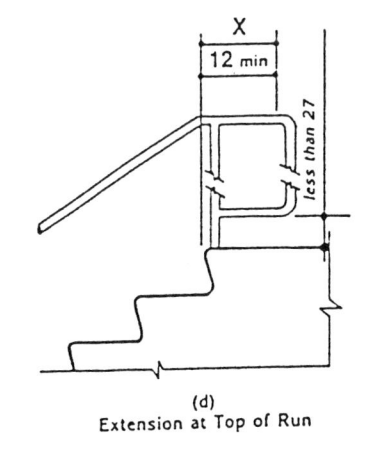

	Yes	No
Ramp	☐	☐
Stairs	☐	☐
Ramp	☐	☐
Stairs	☐	☐

Handrail Extensions

(c) Extension at Bottom of Run

(d) Extension at Top of Run

NOTE:
X is the 12 in minimum handrail extension required at each top riser.

Y is the minimum handrail extension of 12 in plus the width of one tread that is required at each bottom riser.

Stair Handrails

112 Self-Evaluation Survey for Public Libraries - ADAAG

Doors [4.13] -- **Note:** Revolving doors or turnstiles are not acceptable as accessible entrances.

Yes	No
☐	☐

29. Do all accessible entrance doors display a sign or sticker with the symbol for accessibility,

   • If other entrances are not accessible, are signs displayed directing people to accessible entrances,   ☐ ☐

   • Are 50% of all public entrances accessible?   ☐ ☐

Action to be taken/Documentation

Time Frame

Progress

Yes	No
☐	☐

30. Do all accessible entrance doors have a clear space of at least 32 inches,

   Note: With the door open 90 degrees measure the distance between the face of the door and the opposite door frame.

   • If you have double leaf doors, if only one door is opened, is there a clear space of at least 32 inches?   ☐ ☐

Please see the drawing on the next page.

Action to be taken/Documentation

Time Frame

Progress

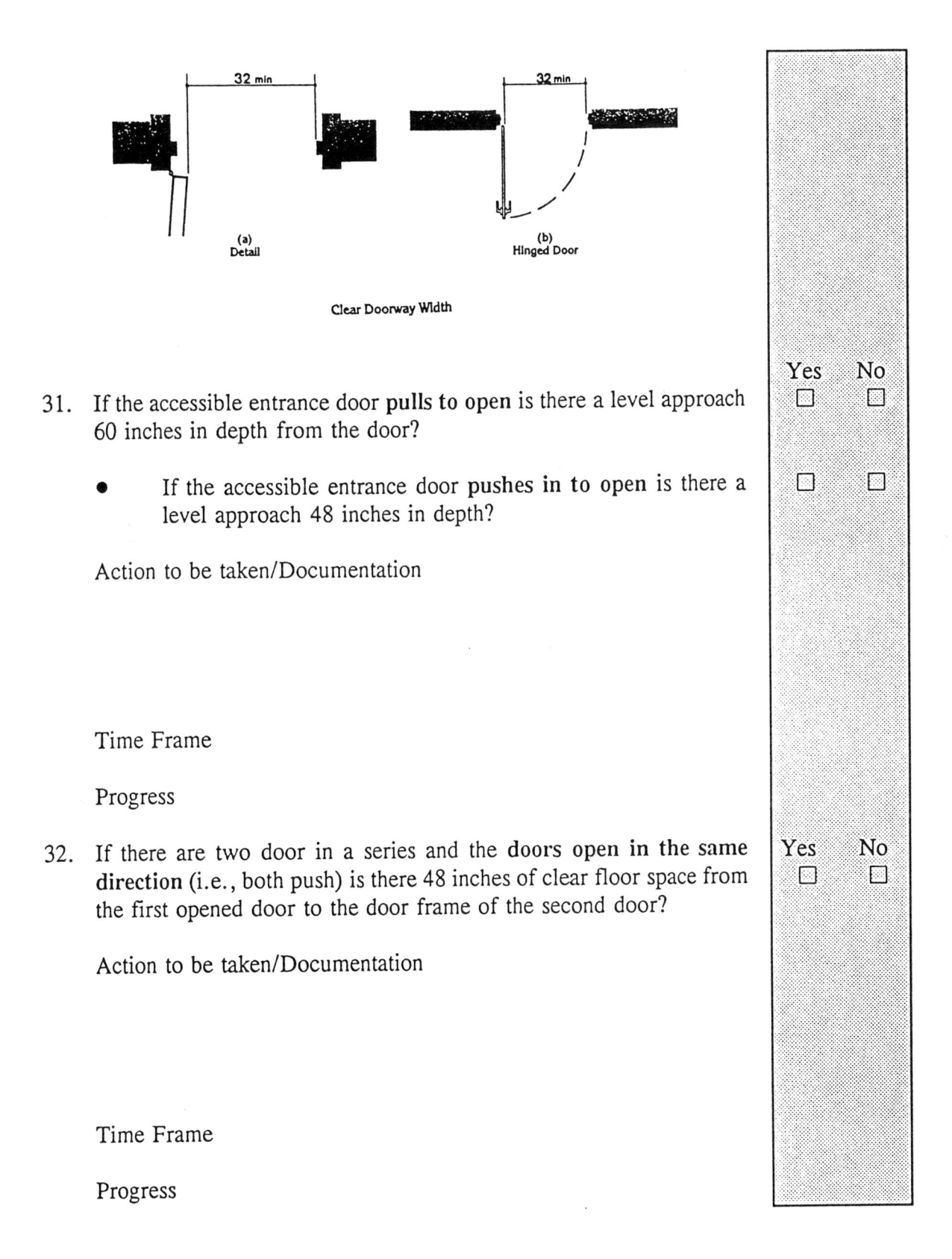

(a) Detail
(b) Hinged Door

Clear Doorway Width

31. If the accessible entrance door **pulls to open** is there a level approach 60 inches in depth from the door?

    Yes ☐ No ☐

    - If the accessible entrance door **pushes in to open** is there a level approach 48 inches in depth?

    Yes ☐ No ☐

    Action to be taken/Documentation

    Time Frame

    Progress

32. If there are two door in a series and the **doors open in the same direction** (i.e., both push) is there 48 inches of clear floor space from the first opened door to the door frame of the second door?

    Yes ☐ No ☐

    Action to be taken/Documentation

    Time Frame

    Progress

33. For two doors in a series and the doors open in opposite directions (one pulling, the second pushing, is there 48 inches of clear space between the doors when they are closed?

   Yes ☐   No ☐

   Action to be taken/Documentation

   Time Frame

   Progress

   Two Hinged Doors in Series

34. Are thresholds of doorways ½ inch or less? **Note:** If existing thresholds are 3/4 inch or less and have (or are modified to have) a beveled edge on each side, they may remain.

   Yes ☐   No ☐

   Action to be taken/Documentation

   Time Frame

   Progress

35. Does the accessible entrance door open with a single effort?   Yes No
    ☐   ☐

    • Is the opening hardware centered at 48 inches from the floor?
    ☐   ☐

    • Is the floor or landing on the inside of the accessible door level?
    ☐   ☐

    Action to be taken/Documentation

    Time Frame

    Progress

Floors [4.5]

                                                                    Yes No
36. Are floor surfaces firm and slip-resistant?   ☐   ☐

    Action to be taken/Documentation

    Time Frame

    Progress

37. If the floor is carpet or carpet tile:

    • is the pile level ½ inch in thickness or less?

    • is carpet secured to the floor?

    • Are exposed edges of carpet fastened to the floor surface and have trim along the entire length of the exposed edge?

    Yes ☐ No ☐
    Yes ☐ No ☐
    Yes ☐ No ☐

    Action to be taken/Documentation

    Time Frame

    Progress

38. If there are any changes in the level of the floors:

    • are they ¼ inch or less?

    • if they are between ¼ and ½ inch, is it beveled with a slope of 1:2? **Note:** If change of level is greater than ½ inch the change is considered a ramp and must comply with Ramps [4.8].

    Yes ☐ No ☐
    ☐ ☐

    Action to be taken/Documentation

    Time Frame

    Progress

Surveying Public Libraries for the ADA

Accessible Routes [4.3]

Please see the drawings on the next page.

39. Is there at least one accessible route connecting accessible buildings, facilities, elements and spaces?

    Yes ☐ No ☐

    Action to be taken/Documentation

    Time Frame

    Progress

40. Does the accessible route have a clear minimum width of 36 inches? **Note:** except for doors which have to have a clear minimum width of 32 inches.

    Yes ☐ No ☐

    Action to be taken/Documentation

    Time Frame

    Progress

41. If the accessible route is less than 60 inches in width, are there passing spaces 60 inches x 60 inches at intervals of not more than 200 ft. **Note:** an intersecting corridor or another accessible route is an acceptable passing space.

    Yes ☐ No ☐

    Action to be taken/Documentation

    Time Frame

    Progress

118 Self-Evaluation Survey for Public Libraries - ADAAG

42. Do the accessible routes have a minimum clear head room of 80 inches?

    Yes ☐ No ☐

    Action to be taken/Documentation

    Time Frame

    Progress

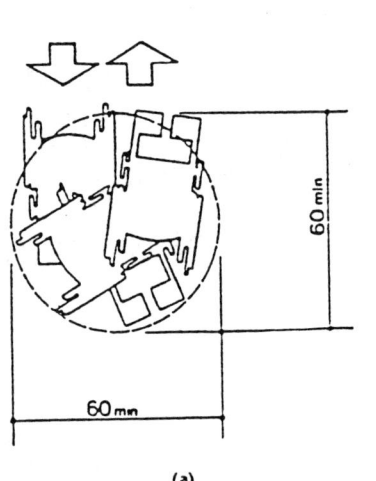

(a) 60-in (1525-mm)-Diameter Space

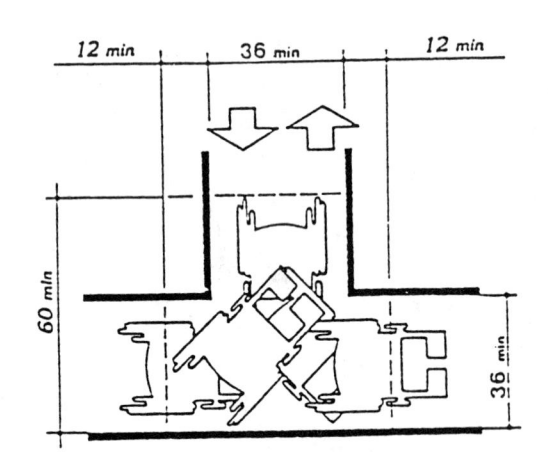

(b) T-Shaped Space for 180° Turns

Protruding Objects [4.4]

Objects projecting from walls (for example: telephones or drinking fountains) are considered protruding objects if they are located on accessible routes.

43. If there are any protruding objects on an accessible route with the leading edges between 27 inches and 80 inches above the floor, are they protruding no more than 4 inches into the accessible route?

    Yes ☐   No ☐

    Action to be taken/Documentation

    Time Frame

    Progress

44. If there are any protruding objects with their lead edges at or below 27 inches, do they leave a minimum clear path of 36 inches?

    Yes ☐   No ☐

    Action to be taken/Documentation

    Time Frame

    Progress

120 Self-Evaluation Survey for Public Libraries - ADAAG

Card Catalogs and Magazine Displays [8.4] - Libraries

45. Do card catalogs and magazine displays have a minimum clear aisle space of 36 inches?

    Action to be taken/Documentation

    Time Frame

    Progress

Yes No
☐ ☐

card catalogs
☐ ☐

magazine display
☐ ☐

46. Is the maximum reach height of card catalogs and magazine displays 48 inches? **Note:** 48 inches is preferred, 54 inches is acceptable.

    Action to be taken/Documentation

    Time Frame

    Progress

Yes No
☐ ☐

card catalogs
☐ ☐

magazine display
☐ ☐

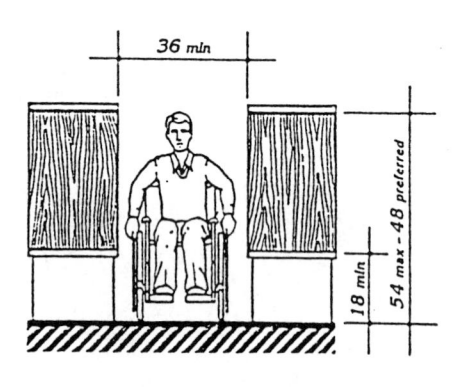

Card Catalog

Book Stacks [8.5]

Note: Shelf height in stack areas is unrestricted.

47. Do stacks have a minimum clear aisle width of 36 inches?
    Note: 42 inches width is preferred.

    Yes ☐   No ☐

    Action to be taken/Documentation

    Time Frame

    Progress

48. Do stacks have a clear space of 36 inches to 48 inches at the ends so a wheelchair can turn corners around stacks?

    Yes ☐   No ☐

    Action to be taken/Documentation

    Time Frame

    Progress

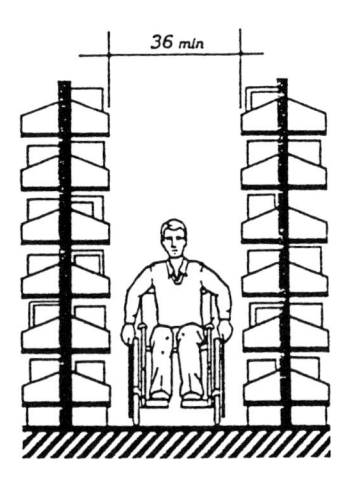

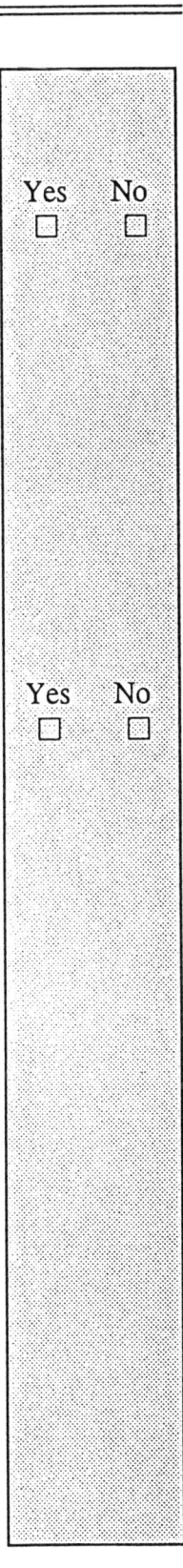

Stacks

Service Counter [8.3]

49. Is there at least one lane or area at each service counter which is accessible,

    Yes ☐ No ☐

    - Is the accessible service counter(s) located on an accessible route(s), and
    - at least 36 inches in length?
    - is the maximum height 36 inches above the finished floor?

    Yes ☐ No ☐
    Yes ☐ No ☐
    Yes ☐ No ☐

    Action to be taken/Documentation

    Time Frame

    Progress

Security System Gates [4.13] -- Note: 4.13 of ADAAG refers to doors. Security gates must comply with the specifications for doors.

50. Do the security gates have a minimum clear opening of 32 inches,

    Yes ☐ No ☐

    - Is the floor space at the security gate(s) level and clear for a minimum of 42 inches for the approach,
    - If the security gate has a threshold, is the threshold ½ inch or less?

    Yes ☐ No ☐
    Yes ☐ No ☐

    Action to be taken/Documentation

    Time Frame

    Progress

Reading and Study Areas [8.2]

Please see the drawing on the next page.

Note: Fixed or built-in seating and tables [4.32]

51. Is at least 5 percent or a minimum of one of each element of fixed seating, tables, or study carrels accessible?

    Yes ☐ No ☐

    Action to be taken/Documentation

    Time Frame

    Progress

52. Is there a clear passage of 36 inches continuous and 32 inches at a point between tables, chairs, or stacks?

    Yes ☐ No ☐

    Action to be taken/Documentation

    Time Frame

    Progress

53. Are there areas of clear space of 60 inches where wheelchairs would need to make 180 degree turns?

    Yes ☐ No ☐

    Action to be taken/Documentation

    Time Frame

    Progress

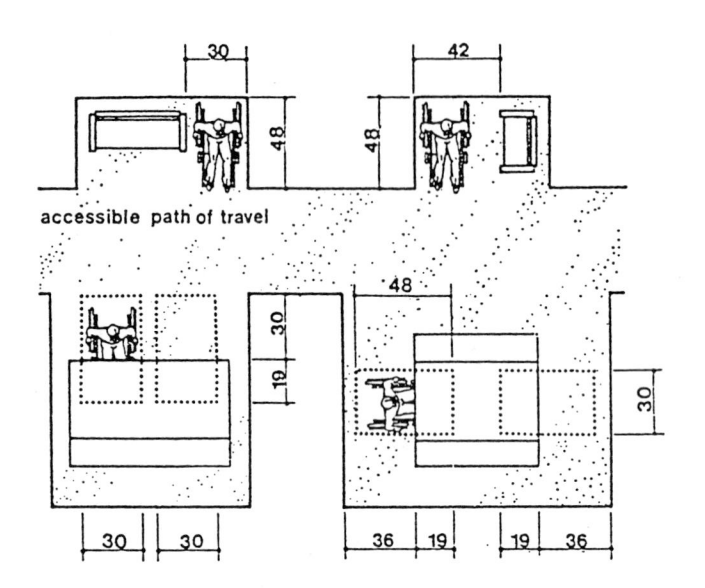

Minimum Clearances for Seating and Tables

54. Are the tables or counters tops of accessible areas between 28 inches to 34 inches above the floor?

   • Is there knee space of 19 inches deep under accessible tables or counters and 27 inches high from the floor to the underside of the tables or counters?

Action to be taken/Documentation

Time Frame

Progress

Yes   No
☐   ☐

☐   ☐

Surveying Public Libraries for the ADA

Assembly Areas and Meeting Rooms [4.1.3(19) and 4.33]

Note: All wheelchair seating is to have a clear view of the stage or front area. Be sure to allow for companion seating in wheelchair areas, as well.

55. Does the assembly area have the correct number of wheelchair locations for seating? See chart.   Yes ☐ No ☐

Capacity of Seating in Assembly Areas	Number of Required Wheelchair Locations
4 to 25	1
26 to 50	2
51 to 300	4
301 to 500	6
over 500	6, plus 1 additional space for for each total seating capacity increase of 100

Action to be taken/Documentation

Time Frame

Progress

56. Does the wheelchair seating adjoin an accessible route that also serves as a means of egress in case of emergency? **Note:** If your meeting and assembly areas have flexible seating for tables and chairs, remember to allow an accessible route 36 inches in width for use in case of emergency.   Yes ☐ No ☐

Action to be taken/Documentation

Time Frame

Progress

57. If the assembly or meeting area has flexible seating, are the tables used for wheelchairs accessible with knee space of 27 inches high, 30 inches wide and 19 inches deep with the table tops 28 inches to 34 inches above the floor?

    Yes ☐ No ☐

    Action to be taken/Documentation

    Time Frame

    Progress

58. In the assembly or meeting area, do the wheelchair accessible spaces have clear floor space 48 inches in length and 66 inches in width for front or rear approaches or 60 inches in length and 66 inches in width for side approaches?

    Yes ☐ No ☐

    Action to be taken/Documentation

    Time Frame

    Progress

Listening Systems [4.33.6 and 4.1.3(19)]

Note: Be sure to check and maintain audible communications and listening systems regularly.

Assistive listening systems are intended to augment standard public address and audio systems. The type of assistive listening system appropriate for a particular application depends on the characteristics of the setting, the nature of the program, and the intended audience. Magnetic induction loops, infra-red and radio frequency systems are types of listening systems which are appropriate for various applications.

59. If the assembly area has fixed seating, is the assistive listening system located within 50 feet of viewing distance of the stage or front area?

    Yes ☐   No ☐

    Action to be taken/Documentation

    Time Frame

    Progress

60. Does the signage include the international symbol of access for hearing loss to notify patrons of the availability of a listening system?

    Yes ☐   No ☐

    Note: Signage for access for hearing loss is in section 4.30 in the ADAAG, and is covered later in the survey.

    Action to be taken/Documentation

    Time Frame

    Progress

Restrooms [4.16, 4.17, 4.18, 4.19, 4.22, 4.24 and 4.26]

Note: If you discover you need to make major changes in the restrooms, be sure you check on state and local codes before final plans are made and work begins.

128 Self-Evaluation Survey for Public Libraries - ADAAG

If your building is older and it is technically infeasible to comply with ADAAG, the installation of at least one unisex restroom per floor, located in the same area as existing restrooms, with appropriate signage (labeling for door and directional signage to the accessible restroom) will be permitted in lieu of modifying existing restrooms [4.1.6(3)(e) in the ADAAG].

This section on restrooms is divided into three parts, to cover the three main types of restrooms:

   restrooms - with stalls
   restrooms - single rooms
   restrooms - unisex

You may want to make copies of these so you can evaluate both male and female facilities, and the restrooms on each floor as well as for separate buildings and branch libraries. Sinks and mirrors are addressed after toilet areas.

Restrooms - With Stalls

Please see drawings on pages 152 and 153.

61. Is the restroom located on an accessible route?   Yes ☐ No ☐

    Action to be taken/Documentation

    Time Frame

    Progress

62. Is there a minimum clearance of 36 inches between all fixtures to an accessible stall?   Yes ☐ No ☐

    Action to be taken/Documentation

    Time Frame

    Progress

63. Is there 60 inches (30 inches radius circle) of clear floor space in the restroom for a wheelchair to make a 180 degree turn?

Yes ☐ No ☐

Action to be taken/Documentation

Time Frame

Progress

64. Is at least one stall accessible and does it display the international symbol of accessibility?

Yes ☐ No ☐

Note: If there are 6 or more stalls, then one additional stall has to be 36 inches wide with an outward swinging, self-closing door and parallel grab bars; on the side walls, 42 inches long, 12 inches from the back wall. Both grab bars must be located between 33 inches and 36 inches from the floor.

Action to be taken/Documentation

Time Frame

Progress

65. Does the immediate area allow 48 inches clear space to approach the stall door? **Note:** If approach is to the latch side of stall door, clear space can be reduced to a 42 inch minimum.

    Yes ☐   No ☐

    Action to be taken/Documentation

    Time Frame

    Progress

66. Does the accessible stall doorway have a minimum of 32 inches clear space?

    Yes ☐   No ☐

    Action to be taken/Documentation

    Time Frame

    Progress

67. Is the accessible stall at least 60 inches wide and 56 inches in length for a wall mounted toilet and 59 inches in length for a floor mounted toilet?

    Yes ☐   No ☐

    Action to be taken/Documentation

    Time Frame

    Progress

68. Does the accessible stall have grab bars which are 1¼ inches to 1½ inches diameter, with a space of 1½ inches between the wall and grab bars? **Note:** If you need to install or replace grab bars please refer to Appendix B of the ADAAG for information on structural strength.

    Yes ☐ No ☐

    Action to be taken/Documentation

    Time Frame

    Progress

69. Is there a grab bar 36 inches long behind (over) the toilet, located 33 inches to 36 inches from the floor and a maximum 6 inches from the closest side wall?

    Yes ☐ No ☐

    Action to be taken/Documentation

    Time Frame

    Progress

70. Is there a grab bar 40 inches long on the side wall closest to the toilet, located 33 inches to 36 inches from the floor and a maximum of 12 inches from the back wall?

    Yes ☐ No ☐

    Action to be taken/Documentation

    Time Frame

    Progress

132 Self-Evaluation Survey for Public Libraries - ADAAG

71. Is the toilet paper holder located within easy reach from the toilet and at least 19 inches from the floor with continuous paper flow?

    Yes ☐ No ☐

    Action to be taken/Documentation

    Time Frame

    Progress

72. Is the toilet seat 17 inches to 19 inches measured from the top of the toilet seat to the floor? **Note:** Toilet seats are not to be spring loaded to return to a lifted position.

    Yes ☐ No ☐

    Action to be taken/Documentation

    Time Frame

    Progress

42 min latch approach only, other approaches 48 min

(a) Standard Stall

(a-1) Standard Stall (end of row)

(c) Rear Wall of Standard Stall

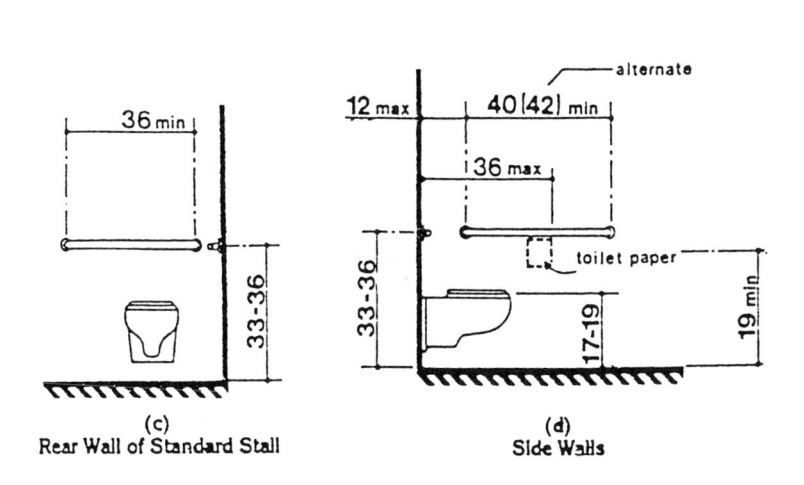

(d) Side Walls

73. Flush controls may be automatic or hand operated. If hand operated, is the flush control mounted on the wide side of the toilet and no more than 44 inches above the floor?

Yes ☐ No ☐

Note: The specifications for flush controls for urinals are the same as for toilets.

Action to be taken/Documentation

Time Frame

Progress

74. For the mens restroom, the urinals may be stall-type or wall hung with an elongated rim:

   Yes   No

   • Is the rim(s) of the accessible urinal(s) 17 inches above the floor?   ☐   ☐

   • Is there clear floor space 30 inches by 48 inches in front of the accessible urinal(s)? **Note:** Urinal shields that do not extend beyond the front edge of the urinal rim may be provided with 29 inches between them.   ☐   ☐

   Action to be taken/Documentation

   Time Frame

   Progress

Restrooms - Single Rooms

   Yes   No

75. Is the restroom located on an accessible route and does it display a sign for accessibility?   ☐   ☐

   Action to be taken/Documentation

   Time Frame

   Progress

76. Is there a clear floor space of at least 48 inches by 56 inches? **Note:** The floor space may include the toilet and be arranged to allow either a left-handed or right-handed approach.

    Yes ☐ No ☐

    Action to be taken/Documentation

    Time Frame

    Progress

77. Is the height of the toilet 17 inches to 19 inches measured to the top of the toilet seat to the floor? **Note:** Toilet seats are not to be spring loaded to return to a lifted position.

    Yes ☐ No ☐

    Action to be taken/Documentation

    Time Frame

    Progress

78. Does the restroom have grab bars 1¼ inches to 1½ inches in diameter with a space of 1½ inches between the wall and grab bars?

    Yes ☐ No ☐

    Action to be taken/Documentation

    Time Frame

    Progress

79. Is there a grab bar behind (over) the toilet at least 36 inches in length and 33 inches to 36 inches from the floor?

    Action to be taken/Documentation

    Time Frame

    Progress

    Yes ☐   No ☐

80. Is there a grab bar on the wall closest to the toilet, 40 inches in length, 33 inches to 36 inches from the floor and 12 inches from the back wall?

    Action to be taken/Documentation

    Time Frame

    Progress

    Yes ☐   No ☐

Clear Floor Space at Water Closets

Grab Bars

81. Flush controls may be automatic or hand operated, if hand operated, is the flush control mounted on the wide side of the toilet and no more than 44 inches above the floor? **Note:** The specifications for flush controls for toilets are the same for urinals.

   Yes No

   Action to be taken/Documentation

   Time Frame

   Progress

82. Is the toilet paper dispenser located within easy reach from the toilet and at least 19 inches from the floor with continuous paper flow?

   Yes No

   Action to be taken/Documentation

   Time Frame

   Progress

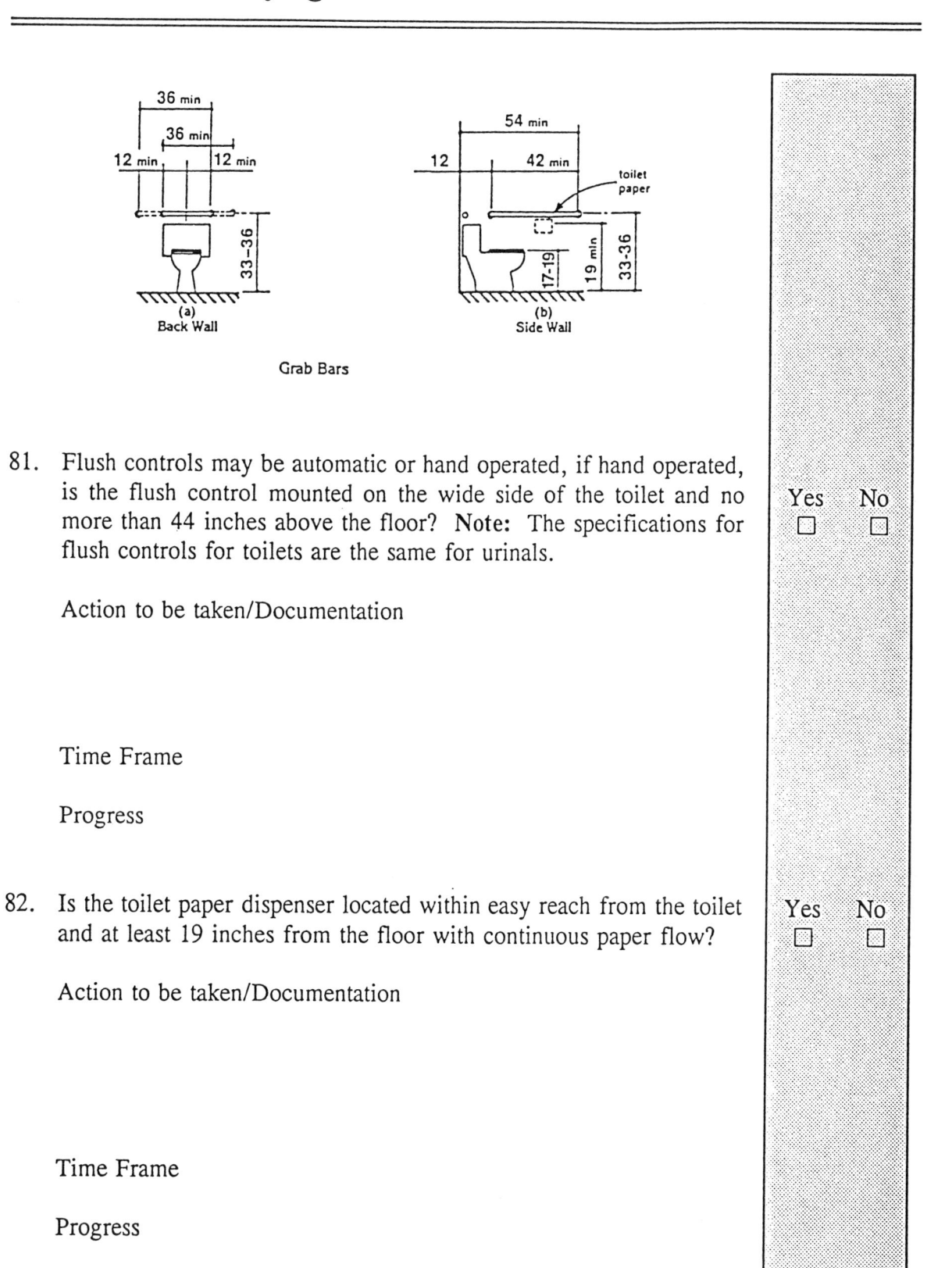

83. For the mens restroom, the urinals may be stall-type or wall hung with an elongated rim:

   Yes   No

- Is the rim(s) of the accessible urinal(s) 17 inches above the floor? ☐ ☐

- Is there clear floor space 30 inches by 48 inches in front of the accessible urinal(s)? ☐ ☐

Note: Urinal shields that do not extend beyond the front edge of the urinal rim may be provided with 29 inches between them.

Action to be taken/Documentation

Time Frame

Progress

Restrooms - Unisex

If you have a unisex accessible restroom it should comply with the survey on restrooms-single rooms. In addition, it should comply with the following questions. There is no requirement for a unisex restroom to have a urinal as well as a toilet.

84. Is the accessible unisex restroom located on an accessible route and in the same area as other restrooms which are not accessible?   Yes ☐   No ☐

Action to be taken/Documentation

Time Frame

Progress

85. Is there signage indicating this is a unisex accessible restroom,   Yes No
    ☐   ☐

    • If the unisex restroom is located near unaccessible restrooms is there signage directing patrons to the accessible unisex restroom?   ☐   ☐

    Action to be taken/Documentation

    Time Frame

    Progress

86. Does the unisex restroom have a privacy latch?   Yes No
    ☐   ☐

    Action to be taken/Documentation

    Time Frame

    Progress

Sinks and Mirrors [4.19 and 4.24]

Please see the drawing on page 161.

Yes No

87. • Are the sink(s) mounted with the rim or counter surface no higher than 34 inches above the floor?   ☐   ☐

    • Is there knee space under the sink 29 inches to the floor and 8 inches deep (from the front rim of the sink)?   ☐   ☐

- Is there toe clearance under the sink 9 inches high from the floor and to the wall?

  Yes ☐ No ☐

  Action to be taken/Documentation

  Time Frame

  Progress

88. Are the hot water and drain pipes under the sink insulated or protected against contact? **Note:** No sharp or abrasive surfaces are allowed under sinks.

    Yes ☐ No ☐

    Action to be taken/Documentation

    Time Frame

    Progress

89. Is there clear floor space of 30 inches by 48 inches in front of a sink? **Note:** The clear floor space can include an accessible route and may include 19 inches in depth under a sink.

    Yes ☐ No ☐

    Action to be taken/Documentation

    Time Frame

    Progress

Surveying Public Libraries for the ADA

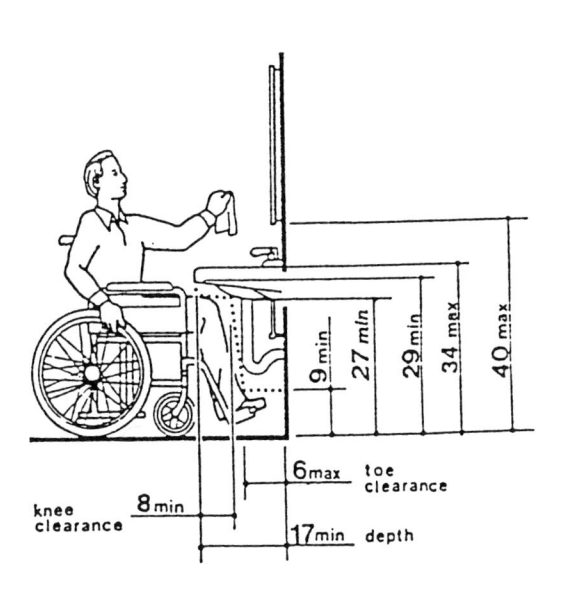

90.
- Are the faucet controls operable with one hand and do not require tight grasping, pinching, or twisting of the wrist? **Note:** Lever-operated, push type, touch type or electronically controlled are acceptable faucet designs.

- If the faucets have automatic shut offs does the water remain on for at least 10 seconds?

Action to be taken/Documentation

Time Frame

Progress

Yes No

91. Are the mirrors mounted with the bottom edge of the reflecting surface no higher than 40 inches above the floor?

    Yes ☐ No ☐

    Action to be taken/Documentation

    Time Frame

    Progress

92. Are the other fixtures in the restroom (i.e., soap dispensers, towels, auto-dryers, sanitary napkin dispensers, waste paper receptacles, etc.) located so the controls or dispensers are at 48 inches maximum from the floor?

    Yes ☐ No ☐

    Action to be taken/Documentation

    Time Frame

    Progress

Water Fountains [4.15]

Where only one water fountain is provided on a floor there is to be one fountain accessible to individuals in wheelchairs and one water fountain for individuals who have difficulty bending or stooping. This can be accomplished by the use of a "hi-lo" fountain or an accessible fountain for wheelchair users and a water cooler.

Surveying Public Libraries for the ADA 143

93. If you have more than one water fountain per floor, are 50% accessible to individuals in wheelchairs,

    Yes No
    ☐ ☐

    • Are accessible water fountains located on an accessible routes? ☐ ☐

    Action to be taken/Documentation

    Time Frame

    Progress

94. Is the spout of the accessible water fountain:

    • no higher than 36 inches measured from the floor to the spout outlet?   Yes No ☐ ☐

    • located on the front of the unit within 3 inches of the front edge?   ☐ ☐

    • adjusted so the flow of water is at least 4 inches high - so a cup or glass can be placed under the flow of water?   ☐ ☐

    Action to be taken/Documentation

    Time Frame

    Progress

144 Self-Evaluation Survey for Public Libraries - ADAAG

95. Are the controls for the accessible water fountain:

    - located on the front or if side mounted, are the controls within 6 inches of the front edge?
    - operable with one hand and does not require a tight grasping, pinching or twisting of the wrist?

    Action to be taken/Documentation

    Time Frame

    Progress

    Yes No
    ☐ ☐

    ☐ ☐

96. If the accessible water fountain is wall or post mounted and has knee space, is the space at least 27 inches high, 30 inches wide, and 17 inches to 19 inches deep?

    Action to be taken/Documentation

    Time Frame

    Progress

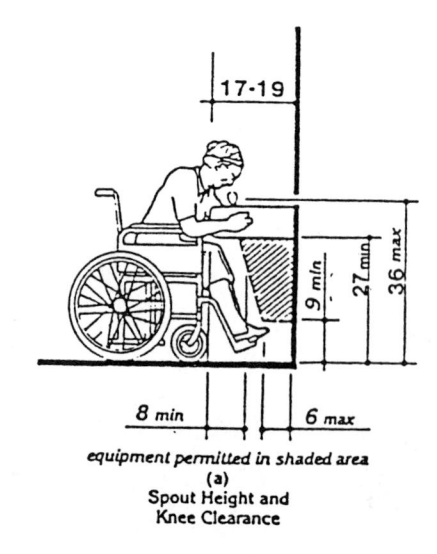

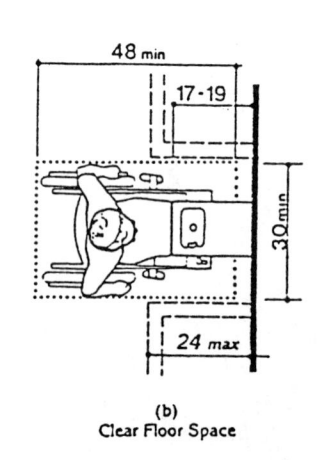

    Yes No
    ☐ ☐

(a) Spout Height and Knee Clearance

(b) Clear Floor Space

Drinking Fountains

97. Is there clear floor space of at least 30 inches wide and 48 inches long in front of the accessible water fountain?

    Yes ☐   No ☐

Action to be taken/Documentation

Time Frame

Progress

Signage [4.30]

Signs which designate permanent rooms and spaces must comply with ADAAG. Directional and informational signage about functional spaces in the building must also comply with ADAAG. Accessible elements (i.e., entrance doors, restrooms, water fountains and parking spaces) must display the International Symbol of Accessibility. Temporary signage, such as building directories, or other temporary information does not have to comply with ADAAG.

Note: Upper and lower case letters are permitted.

98. Do all signs which are required to comply with ADAAG have a width-to-height ratio between 3:5 and 1:1 for letters and numbers?

    Yes ☐   No ☐

Action to be taken/Documentation

Time Frame

Progress

99. Do the individual letters and numbers of the signs which have to comply with ADAAG have a stroke width-to-height ratio between 1:5 and 1:10?

   Yes ☐ No ☐

   Action to be taken/Documentation

   Time Frame

   Progress

100. If signs are placed overhead (minimum 80 inches above the floor), are the letters and numbers at least 3 inches in height?

   Yes ☐ No ☐

   Please see page 167.

   Action to be taken/Documentation

   Time Frame

   Progress

101. Are permanent signs for rooms and spaces installed on the wall adjacent to the latch side of the door and mounted at 60 inches above the floor to the centerline of the sign? **Note:** If there is no wall space on the latch side of the door, including double leaf doors, the sign should be placed on the nearest adjacent wall.

   Yes ☐ No ☐

   Please see the drawing on page 167.

   Action to be taken/Documentation

   Time Frame

   Progress

Display Conditions
International Symbol of Accessibility

International TDD Symbol

International Symbol of Access for Hearing Loss

102. Can the permanent signs be approached by a person without encountering a protruding object or stand within the area of a swing door?

Yes ☐   No ☐

Action to be taken/Documentation

Time Frame

Progress

103. Are the letters and numbers of permanent signs:

- at least 5/8 inch but no more than 2 inches in height?
- raised 1/32 inch?
- accompanied by Grade 2 Braille? **Note:** Grade 2 Braille refers to the spelling of words and use of contractions.

Yes ☐   No ☐
☐   ☐
☐   ☐

Action to be taken/Documentation

Time Frame

Progress

104. If pictograms are used for permanent signs, is the verbal equivalent placed directly below the pictogram? **Note:** Signs with pictograms should be at least 6 inches high.

   Yes ☐   No ☐

   Action to be taken/Documentation

   Time Frame

   Progress

105. • Are the characters and backgrounds of permanent signs a flat, matte, or other non-glare finish?

   Yes ☐   No ☐

   • Do the characters contrast in color with the background of permanent signs? **Note:** The signs should have light colored characters on a dark background or dark characters on a light background.

   ☐   ☐

   Action to be taken/Documentation

   Time Frame

   Progress

Controls and Operating Mechanisms [4.27]

Electrical switches and receptacles, dispensers and other operable equipment. **Note:** These requirements do not apply where the use of special equipment dictates otherwise or where electrical and communications systems are not normally intended for use by building occupants. This section may only apply to restrooms (light switches and dispensers) and meeting rooms (light switches and receptacles, heat and A/C control, communication system receptacles).

106. Is there clear floor space to approach controls - forward approach 30 inches wide and 48 inches deep, parallel approach 48 inches wide and 30 inches deep? Yes ☐ No ☐

    Action to be Taken/Documentation

    Time Frame

    Progress

107. Is the maximum height of light switches and dispensers 48 inches from the floor? Yes ☐ No ☐

    Action to be Taken/Documentation

    Time Frame

    Progress

108. Are wall mounted electrical and communication system receptacles mounted no less than 15 inches above the floor?

    Yes ☐ No ☐

    Action to be Taken/Documentation

    Time Frame

    Progress

Lifts and Elevators [4.11 and 4.10]

Note: If your library is considering a wheelchair lift, the lift will have to comply with state and local codes as well as the American National Standards Institute (ANSI) A17.1 Safety Code for Elevators and Escalators, Section XX, 1990, and ADAAG. The ADAAG requires lifts to allow unassisted entry, operation and exit from the lift, as well as meet minimum clear floor space and stable, slip resistant floor and threshold requirements.

109. Is the accessible elevator or lift located on an accessible route?

    Yes ☐ No ☐

    Action to be Taken/Documentation

    Time Frame

    Progress

Surveying Public Libraries for the ADA

Elevators: Please check the following features to be sure they are in working order. IF the elevator needs repairs or improvements, refer to the ADAAG 4.10 Elevators and your service technician.

		Yes	No
Call Buttons:	• centered at 42 inches above the floor	☐	☐
	• have a visual signal when call is registered and answered	☐	☐
	• button size 3/4 inch in smallest dimension	☐	☐
Hall Lanterns:	• mounted 72 inches to the centerline above the floor	☐	☐
	• have a visual and audible signal	☐	☐
	• visual elements at least 2½ inches at the smallest dimension	☐	☐
Floor Designators	• located on both door jams 60 inches on centerline above the floor.	☐	☐
	• raised numbers 2 inches high and braille for the floors	☐	☐
Doors	• 36 inches clear space	☐	☐
	• open and close automatically	☐	☐
	• If obstructed - door stops and reopen	☐	☐
	• reopening device hold door open for 20 seconds before closing.	☐	☐
Elevator Car	• automatic self-leveling feature	☐	☐
	• clear floor space 54 inches by 68 inches	☐	☐
	• visual car position indicator	☐	☐
Control Panel	• buttons at least 3/4 inch in smallest dimension	☐	☐
	• buttons designated by Braille and raised alphabet and numbers	☐	☐
	• buttons provide a visual indicator	☐	☐
	• buttons no higher than 54 inches	☐	☐
	• emergency controls grouped at bottom with centerlines no less than 35 inches	☐	☐

Safety Alarms [4.28]

Note: If emergency warning systems are provided, they must include both audible and visual alarms.

110. If there is an emergency warning system (fire alarms), are visual signal appliances provided in restrooms, general usage areas (meeting rooms), hallways, lobbies, and other areas for common use?

    Yes ☐ No ☐

    Action to be Taken/Documentation

    Time Frame

    Progress

111. Is the visual signal a xenon strobe type lamp or equivalent?

    Yes ☐ No ☐

    Action to be Taken/Documentation

    Time Frame

    Progress

112. Is the visual signal appliance placed 80 inches above the floor or 6 inches below the ceiling, which ever is lower?

    Yes ☐ No ☐

    Action to be Taken/Documentation

    Time Frame

    Progress

Public Telephones [4.31]

Note: Most pay telephones which were installed after 1987 are wheelchair accessible. If the pay phones at your library do not meet ADA requirements notify the telephone company so they can arrange to lower or install an accessible pay phone.

113. If public telephones are provided, is the required number of wheelchair accessible public telephones present? See chart.

    Yes ☐ No ☐

Number of each type of telephone provided on each floor	Number of telephone required to comply
1 or more single units	1 per floor
1 bank	1 per floor
2 or more banks	1 per floor

    Note: A bank consists of two or more adjacent public telephones.

    Action to be Taken/Documentation

    Time Frame

    Progress

114. Are accessible pay telephones located on an accessible route with minimum clear floor space of 30 inches by 48 inches in front of the accessible telephones?

    Yes ☐ No ☐

    Action to be Taken/Documentation

    Time Frame

    Progress

115. Is the highest operable part of the accessible pay telephone 48 inches above the floor for front approach or 54 inches above the floor for a parallel approach?

    Yes ☐   No ☐

    Action to be Taken/Documentation

    Time Frame

    Progress

116. Are accessible pay telephones:

    - hearing aid compatible,

    - identified by the symbol of accessibility?

    Yes ☐   No ☐
    Yes ☐   No ☐

    Action to be Taken/Documentation

    Time Frame

    Progress

117. Do accessible pay telephones have push button controls where service for such equipment is available?

    Yes ☐   No ☐

    Action to be Taken/Documentation

    Time Frame

    Progress

118. Is the cord from the accessible pay telephone to the handset at least 29 inches in length?

   Action to be Taken/Documentation

   Yes ☐ No ☐

   Time Frame

   Progress

Text Telephones (TDD) For Public Pay Telephones [4.31.9]

Note: If the total number of four or more public pay telephones (including interior and exterior phones) is provided at a site, and at least one is an interior telephone, then at least one interior public text telephone shall be provided.

119. When the text telephone used with a pay telephone is permanent is it attached within, or adjacent to, the telephone enclosure?

   Yes ☐ No ☐

   - If the pay telephone is designed to accommodate a portable text telephone, is there a shelf and an electrical outlet within or adjacent to the telephone enclosure? **Note:** The telephone handset must be able to be placed flush on the surface of the shelf and the self must be able to accommodate a text telephone and allow a minimum of 6 inches vertical clearance in the area where the text telephone is to be placed.

   Yes ☐ No ☐

   Action to be Taken/Documentation

   Time Frame

   Progress

120. If an acoustic coupler is used, is the telephone cord long enough to connect the text telephone and the telephone receiver?

    Action to be Taken/Documentation

    Yes ☐ No ☐

    Time Frame

    Progress

121. Is the signage which displays the international TDD symbol on the text telephone?

    Action to be Taken/Documentation

    Yes ☐ No ☐

    Time Frame

    Progress

APPENDIX B
Adaptive Technology Exhibitors

Assistive Technology
2791-F N. Texas St.
Suite 257
Fairfield, CA 94533
(707) 864-6321

G. David Childers & Assoc.
Products for the Blind & Low Vision
 (Optelec USA, Inc., and Xerox Imaging
 Systems/Kurzweil Personal Reader)
6879 Annapolis Quay Circle
Stockton, CA 95219
(209) 472-1479

Descriptive Video Service
WGBH
124 Western Ave.
Boston, MA 02134
(617) 492-2777 ext. 3490

E-Z Reader, Inc.
3920 Central Ave.
St. Petersburg, FL 33711
(800) 275-7232

Gaylord Bros.
Box 4901
Syracuse, NY 13221-4901
(315) 457-5070

Golden Gate Hearing Services
1833 Fillmore St., Suite 100
San Francisco, CA 94115
(415) 931-8180

Highsmith Company
W. 5527 Highway 106E
Fort Atkinson, WI 53538
(414) 563-9571

HumanWare, Inc. [Attn: Rick Plescia]
6245 King Rd.
Loomis, CA 95650
(800) 722-3393

Kroy, Inc.
14555 N. Hayden Rd.
Scottsdale, AZ 85260
(800) 733-KROY

Mentor O & O
3000 Longwater Dr.
Norwell, MA 10161-1672
(800) 992-7557

Pacific Bell
Deaf & Disabled Services
2850 Telegraph Ave.
Berkeley, CA 94705
(510) 644-7524

Phonic Ear, Inc.
3880 Cypress Dr.
Petaluma, CA 94954
(800) 227-0735

Rebus Institute
198 Taylor Blvd., Suite 201
Millbrae, CA 94030
(415) 697-7424

Telesensory Systems, Inc.
455 North Bernardo Ave.
Mountain View, CA 94039
(800) 227-8418

University Copy Service
2411 West Bond
University Park, IL 60466
(800) 762-2736

The Worden Company
199 E. 17th St.
Holland, MI 49423
(800) 748-0561

APPENDIX C

Ten Commandments of Etiquette for Communicating with Persons with Disabilities

1. When talking with a person with a disability, speak directly to that person rather than through a companion or sign language interpreter.
2. When introduced to a person with a disability, it is appropriate to offer to shake hands. People with limited hand use or who wear an artificial limb can usually shake hands. (Shaking hands with the left hand is an acceptable greeting.)
3. When meeting a person with a visual impairment, always identify yourself and others who may be with you. When conversing in a group, remember to identify the person to whom you are speaking.
4. If you offer assistance, wait until the offer is accepted. Then listen to, or ask for, instructions.
5. Treat adults as adults. Address people who have disabilities by their first names only when extending the same familiarity to all others. (Never patronize people who use wheelchairs by patting them on the head or shoulder.)
6. Leaning or hanging on a person's wheelchair is similar to leaning or hanging on a person, and is generally considered annoying. The chair is part of the personal body space of the person who uses it.
7. Listen attentively when you're talking with a person who has difficulty speaking. Be patient and wait for the person to finish, rather than correcting or speaking for the person. If necessary, ask short questions that require short answers, a nod or shake of the head. Never pretend to understand if you are having difficulty doing so. Instead, repeat what you have understood and allow the person to respond. The response will clue in and guide your understanding.
8. When speaking with a person in a wheelchair or a person who uses crutches, place yourself at eye level in front of the person to facilitate the conversation.
9. To get the attention of a person who is hearing impaired, tap the person on the shoulder or wave your hand. Look directly at the person and speak clearly, slowly, and expressively to determine if the person can read your lips. Not all people with a hearing impairment can lip read. For those who do not read lips, be sensitive to their needs by placing yourself so that you face the light source and keep hands, cigarettes, and food away from your mouth when speaking.
10. Relax. Don't be embarrassed if you happen to use accepted, common expressions such as "See you later," or "Did you hear about this?" that seem to relate to a person's disability.

Reprinted with the permission of the National Center for Access Unlimited, 155 N. Wacker Drive, Suite 315, Chicago, IL 60605; (312) 368-0380 V; (312) 368-0179 TTD.

APPENDIX D

Exemplary Library Programs and Services for People with Disabilities— A Sampling in June 1992

LIBRARY	PROGRAMS AND SERVICES	CONTACT
Scottsdale Public Library, Arizona	Citizen committee to implement the ADA in libraries	Connie Mulholland, Library Manager
Montgomery County Public Libraries, Rockville, Maryland	Two-tiered approach to comprehensive service	Agnes Griffen, Director
Phoenix Public Library, Arizona	Special Needs Center approach to comprehensive service	Cindi Holt, Supervisor, Special Needs Center
Berkeley Public Library, California	"If you can't come to us, we'll come to you!"	Regina Minudri, Director of Library Services
Los Angeles Public Library, California	Services to shut-ins	Thomas E. Alford, Assistant City Librarian
Pioneer Library System, Newark, New York	Bridges to the community	Patricia Stocker, Outreach Coordinator
The Free Library of Philadelphia	The GED program	Vicki Lange Collins
San Diego Public Library, California	I CAN! Center	Judith G. Castiano, Outreach Services Library
The New York Public Library, New York City	*Making Contact: A Guide for Library Staff Serving Patrons with Disabilities*	Mildred Dotson, Coordinator, Special Services
Seattle Public Library, Washington	Library equal access program	Cleo B. Kelly, Coordinator (LEAP)
San Francisco Public Library, California	Services for the deaf and hearing impaired	Marti Goddard, Librarian for the Services
Ramapo College of New Jersey, Manwah	Barrier-free campus	Norman N. Yueh, Director, Library Service
Appalachian State University, Boone, North Carolina	Resource guide for students with disabilities	Pat Farthing, Librarian, Instructional Materials
Vermont State Library, Montpelier	Planning for accessibility	Patricia E. Klinck, State Librarian

LIBRARY	PROGRAMS AND SERVICES	CONTACT
State Library of Pennsylvania, Harrisburg	Computerized "wellness stations"	Stephen Mallinger, Library Development
Utah State Library, Salt Lake City	Volunteer program	Gerald Buttars, Director
Memphis/Shelby County Public Library, Tennessee	WYPL— an open-air channel	Judy Drescher
Public Library of Nashville/Davidson County, Tennessee	WPLN— 24 hours per day, year-round broadcasts	Caroline Stark
Worcester County Library, Snow Hill, Maryland	Active communication with the patron	Stewart L. Wells, Director
Onandaga County Public Library, Syracuse, New York	Helping hand: deaf awareness	Rodmilla Tuttle
Robinson Township Public Library District, Illinois	"Talking computer" access for visually impaired students	Shirley Wakefield, Director
Jefferson–Madison Regional Library, Charlottesville, North Carolina	Adults who are mentally retarded use the library	Donna M. Selle, Director
North Suburban Library System, Wheeling, Illinois	Skokie Accessible Library project: "SALS"	Elliot E. Kanner, Resource Coordinator
Hennepin County Library, Minnetonka, Minnesota	Interpreted children's summer program	Eileen Cavanaugh, Program Office
Pikes Peak Library District, Colorado Springs	Challenged children's reading center	Nancy Downs, Officer of Public Information
Atlanta–Fulton Public Library, Atlanta, Georgia	Learning center for test preparation, adult literacy, visual/hearing areas	Sylvia Cordell, Manager, Learning Center
Cleveland Public Library, Ohio	CD-ROM reference for people who are blind/visually handicapped	Barbara Mates

Compiled by Phyllis I. Dalton, Library Consultant, 7090 E. Mescal St. #261, Scottsdale, AZ 85254; (602) 951-7361.

APPENDIX E

The Americans with Disabilities Act

NIDRR ADA Technical Assistance Initiative

The National Institute on Disability and Rehabilitation Research (NIDRR) of the U.S. Department of Education has funded a network of fifteen grantees to provide information, training, and technical assistance to businesses and agencies with duties and responsibilities under the ADA and to people with disabilities who have rights under the Act. There are ten regional Disability and Business Technical Assistance Centers, three Materials Development Projects (two for employment and one for public accommodation/accessibility), and two National Training Projects, a peer and family training network and a local capacity-building program for independent living centers.

Regional Disability and Business
Technical Assistance Centers
(DBTACs)
1-800-949-4232 Voice/TDD

If you need information or technical assistance on the ADA, contact the center in your region. When you dial the toll-free number above, your free call will automatically ring through to the NIDRR DBTAC responsible for the region of the country that contains the area code you are calling from.

Region 1 (CT, ME, MA, NH, RI, VT)
New England DBTAC
145 Newbury St.
Portland, ME 04101
(207) 874-6535 Voice/TDD

Region 2 (NJ, NY, PR, VI)
Northeast DBTAC
United Cerebral Palsy Association
 of New Jersey
354 South Broad St.
Trenton, NJ 08608
(609) 392-4004 Voice
(609) 392-7044 TDD

Region 3 (DE, DC, MD, PA, VA, WV)
Mid-Atlantic DBTAC
 Endependence Center of Northern Virginia
2111 Wilson Blvd., Suite 400
Arlington, VA 22201
(703)525-3268 Voice/TDD

Region 4 (AL, FL, GA, KY, MS, NC, SC, TN)
Southeast DBTAC
United Cerebral Palsy Association, Inc./
 National Alliance of Business
1776 Peachtree St., Suite 310 North
Atlanta, GA 30309
(404) 888-0022 Voice
(404) 888-9098 TDD

Region 5 (IL IN MI, MN, OH, WI)
Great Lakes DBTAC
University oi Illinois at Chicago/UAP
1640 W. Roosevelt Rd. M/C627
Chicago, IL 60608
(312) 413-7756 Voice/TDD

Region 6 (AR, LA, NM, OK, TX)
Southwest DBTAC
Independent Living Research Utilization/

The Institute for Rehabilitation and Research
2323 S. Shepherd St., Suite 1000
Houston, TX 77019
(713) 520-0232 Voice
(713) 520-5136 TDD

Region 7 (IA, KS, NB, MO)
Great Plains DBTAC
University of Missouri at Columbia
4816 Santana Drive
Columbia, MO 65203
(314) 882-3600 Voice/TDD

Region 8 (CO, MT, ND, SD, UT, WY)
Rocky Mountain DBTAC
Meeting the Challenge, Inc.
3630 Sinton Rd., Suite 103
Colorado Springs, CO 80907-5072
(719) 444-0252 Voice/TDD

Region 9 (AZ, CA, HI, NV, Pacific Basin)
Pacific DBTAC
Berkeley Planning Associates
440 Grand Ave., Suite 500
Oakland, CA 94610
(510) 465-7884 Voice
(510) 465-3172 TDD

Region 10 (AK, ID, OR, WA)
Northwest DBTAC
Washington State Governor's Committee
P.O. Box 9046
Olympia, WA 98507-9046
(206) 438-3168 Voice
(206) 438-3167 TDD

Materials Development Projects

NOTE: The Materials Development Projects are funded only to develop, test, and design materials, not to provide training or technical assistance. The materials generated by them will be produced and distributed through the other NIDRR grantees, any of whom can provide information as to what is available and what is forthcoming.

Employment

Cornell University
School of Industrial & Labor Relations
106 Extension
Ithaca, NY 14853-3901

International Association of Machinists
Center for Administration, Rehabilitation, and Employment Services
1300 Connecticut Ave., NW, Suite 912
Washington, DC 20036

Public Accommodation/Accessibility

Barrier Free Environments, Inc.
Water Garden
Highway 70 West
P.O. Box 30634
Raleigh, NC 27622

National Training Projects

Parent Information Center
151A Manchester St.
P.O. Box 1422
Concord, NH 03301
(603) 224-7005 Voice/TDD

National Council on Independent Living
3607 Chapel Rd.
Newton Square, PA 19073
(215) 353-6066 Voice
(215) 353-6083 TDD

National ADA Technical Assistance Grants Coordinator

Abt Associates Inc.
55 Wheeler St.
Cambridge, MA 02138
(617) 492-7100 Voice
(617) 354-6618 TDD

Federal Contacts for ADA Information

Equal Employment Opportunity Commission
1801 L St., NW
Washington, DC 20507
(800) USA-EEOC Voice
(202) 663-4494 TDD

U.S. Department of Justice
Civil Rights Division
Coordination and Review Section
P.O. Box 66118
Washington, DC 20035-6118
(202) 514-0301 Voice
(202) 514-0381 TDD
(202) 514-0383 TDD

U.S. Architectural and Transportation
 Barriers Compliance Board
1331 F St., NW, Suite 1000
Washington, DC 20004-1111
(800) USA-ABLE Voice
(202) 272-5449 TDD

The President's Committee on Employment
 of People with Disabilities
1331 F St., NW, Third Floor
Washington, DC 20004-1107
(202) 376-6200 Voice
(202) 376-6205 TDD

Disability and Business Technical Assistance Centers

The ten regional Disability and Business Technical Assistance Centers focus on providing, within their respective regions, information and technical assistance to employers and other covered entities, as well as to persons with disabilities, to facilitate appropriate implementation of the ADA, successful employment outcomes for individuals with disabilities, and greater accessibility in public accommodations. In addition, the DBTACs will develop information resources, databases, reference guides, and expert consultant pools that will serve as resources for implementation of the technical assistance programs.

National Peer Training Projects

The two National Peer Training Projects conduct training in order to enhance the capacity of persons with disabilities and their organizations to facilitate the implementation of the ADA. One NTP is focused on peer training of Independent Living Center staff, associates, and volunteers. The other NTP is focused on developing a peer and family training network in which individuals with disabilities or their parents or other family members will provide training to their peers throughout the country.

Materials Development Projects

These three projects develop and test technical assistance and training materials and programs, for use by the DBTACs and NTPs. Two of the MDPs' focus is primarily on employment issues, developing training programs, materials and resources, or repackaging existing materials. The other MDP's focus is on accessibility and public accommodations, developing or identifying and adapting self-administered survey guides, checklists, materials with information on design alternatives that can be used by the target audiences to evaluate and create accessible environments.

Preparation of this publication was supported by the National Institute on Disability and Rehabilitation Research of the U.S. Department of Education under Contract No. HN91041001.